Dummy

Other books by Ernest Tidyman:

SHAFT
ABSOLUTE ZERO
SHAFT AMONG THE JEWS
SHAFT'S BIG SCORE
SHAFT HAS A BALL
THE GANG'S ALL HERE, SHAFT
HIGH PLAINS DRIFTER

Dummy

ERNEST TIDYMAN

W. H. Allen
London and New York
A division of Howard & Wyndham Ltd
1974

© Ernest Tidyman 1974

First British edition 1974

This book or parts thereof may

not be reproduced in any form

without permission in writing.

Printed in Great Britain by Northumberland Press Ltd, Gateshead

for the Publishers, W. H. Allen & Co. Ltd,

44 Hill Street, London W1X 8LB

Bound by Richard Clay (The Chaucer Press) Ltd,

Bungay, Suffolk

ISBN 0 491 01392 2

Introduction

This is neither a plea for sympathy for Donald Lang nor a justification of him. He is in his middle twenties as this is written and has spent one-fourth of his life behind bars. He has been accused of two murders and suspected of involvement in others.

'I don't know about The Dummy,' a Chicago detective said during the research for this book, 'but every time he goes through a neighbourhood we find a dead broad.'

He is a suspect personality.

But Donald Lang is also deaf, mute, illiterate, probably in-educable now, possibly psychotic and perhaps brain-damaged by disease and accident in childhood. He is also an American black, which is considered an infirmity and a defect by a serious segment of the community.

He is nothing and nobody; he will never be anything or anybody. That may be the reason he is worth thinking about.

Given the intelligence, resourcefulness, generosity and concern of his fellow men, one for the other, Donald Lang might have been.

That is the tragedy.

Ernest Tidyman
15 July 1973

CHAPTER I

Saturday morning, 12 November 1965. A cold, black moment when most of Chicago slept. The lakefront wind, a wind called *the wolf* by old jazz musicians, found a place to howl along Washburne Avenue, at the mouth of the alley that separated it from Roosevelt Road on Chicago's Near West Side.

Mrs. Mamie Harris, a thirty-two-year-old black woman, left her apartment on the second floor of the time-stained brick building at 1652 Washburne at 6 a.m. Her purpose was to carry the previous day's garbage and trash to the night depository in the alley, where the riches of the ghetto had accumulated for years and gathered an interest in debris, some of it human. She walked through the gangway between her building and 1654 Washburne, until she reached the door of the latter building. She found the body there, choked back a scream of shock and fear and ran to call the police.

The language of the first report was as cold and dark as the early winter morning :

'Victim was found lying on her right side at the bottom of a cement stairway behind a partially open door. The door leads to a gangway on ground level. The stairway leads to a second floor and is between a two-flat building and a garage which roof serves as a back porch. Victim was battered about the head and suffered excessive bleeding from the mouth. Victim's red ski type pants and panties were down below her knees. Her upper torso was bare and her red sweater was found beneath her body. There was a large quantity of blood, partially coagulated, around the upper part of her body and a small amount splashed on the stairs.'

There was no mystery about how she had come to this conclusion of life. She was identified by her brother as Mrs.

7

Ernestine Williams, thirty-eight. She had lived nearby, and the police described her as a 'known prostitute.' The body was taken to the Cook County Morgue, identified again by the brother for the endless legalities of death, and pronounced officially dead by Z. Solbos, M.D. A post mortem examination was performed by E. Tapia, M.D., Coroner's Pathologist. Stated cause of death was Stab Wound in Lungs. Cuttings were made of nails and hair. Swabs were taken from all the orifices of the body to determine if the assault had been sexual as well as homicidal. What remained of the body was released to an undertaker for the dignity of burial.

So frequent and so routine were the elements of this murder in the daily life of Chicago—in June or January as well as on any 12 November in any year—that the rest of the city's 3⅓ million inhabitants did not notice the violent passing of Ernestine Williams. But here, in horror and boredom, was the genesis of a murder case like no other in the land and legal questions that could not be answered by courts or Constitution.

Such considerations, present or future, did not concern the police, whose area of responsibility in the American system was sharply limited. A body rendered lifeless by personal violence—find the killer. The trail is fresh and hopefully uncluttered. Routine work, success indicated.

The investigation was conducted by a calm and intelligent veteran, Detective Sergeant Louis Denson, Area 4, Homicide; a huge, muscular black man who had worked Chicago's Near West Side for many years and knew it as well as the animal who survives the jungle knows both killer and prey.

'We get a murder a night around here. Bottle gangs, winos, half-crazy hopheads. The week before this case I found a woman's head in a garbage can, the rest of her down the alley. Same alley that runs between the Romeo Bar and where we found the body of Ernestine Williams. A guy takes a chance if he pulls out five bucks and shows it. He might not get home that night.'

Denson, with his intimate knowledge of the neighbourhood's prostitution patterns, had no difficulty retracing Mrs. Williams' progress of the night before. He crossed the alley to the rear entrance of the Romeo Tavern at Roosevelt Road and Paulina Street. At night, the Romeo teemed with activity and a number of prostitutes used it for pastime and the business of pleasure. In daytime the Romeo was quiet, half-somnolent.

Denson sent word for the owner, Bernard Levi, and the night bartender to appear. But while the detective was casting an official pall over the mood of the place, a customer named Lee Jackson drifted in. He had been there the night before, knew Ernestine Williams, and had seen her drinking with a young, black man. Jackson said the young man was quiet and just made gestures at people rather than talking to them, and seemed to be known to the bartender and maybe some others. Jackson had even been talking with Mrs. Williams. Before she left she told Jackson she would buy him a beer and he waited around but she didn't come back. He also provided the names of a couple of women who had talked to Ernestine that night in the Romeo.

Denson had officers interview Mrs. Dorothy Hunter at her home at 1634 Washburne :

'Ernestine was dressed all in red. She loved that colour. She had a red sweater and red pants, everything red. The man was wearing a light-coloured jacket. She had a red coat, but she didn't have it when she walked out of the Romeo with this man. She gave it to her friend, Mary Jane Carter, to hold for her.'

The police then called on Mrs. Carter at the address furnished by Mrs. Hunter, 1625 West 13th Street. She described a young man, as Lee Jackson had, and said he had approached Mrs. Williams while she was dancing. He showed Mrs. Williams some money and motioned for her to accompany him out of the place. Ernestine gave her the red coat, Mrs. Carter said, and told her to keep it until she returned. Later, Mrs. Carter said, the man returned to the Romeo, approached her and pointed to the red coat. He made motions towards the alley, as if he wished to take the coat to Mrs. Williams. Mrs. Carter said she refused to give the coat to the young man and, in fact, had brought it home for safekeeping.

As the day wore on at the Romeo, it was determined that Mrs. Williams' companion of the night before was a young man named Donald Lang, also called 'The Dummy'. Denson was encouraged. No reason to rush. He worked carefully and thoroughly in collecting information, before he moved to arrest Donald Lang and order an investigation at Lang's place of residence, 1440 West 14th Street, one of the ABLA Housing Project buildings. He had also learned where Donald worked.

Denson drove to the huge produce trucking area of South

9

Water Market and found the office of the Harper Motor Van Lines. Sid Harper said that Donald Lang had been there on time that morning, working day-to-day as a freight handler, and had gone with a driver to unload a truck at the Campbell Soup Company at 2700 West 35th Street. That's where Denson got his first look at his suspect. Donald was unloading heavy bags and crates with remarkable ease and dexterity. He looked much younger than his age—twenty—maybe sixteen or seventeen.

'A well put together kid, though not big,' said Denson. 'Very strong.'

Denson arrested and handcuffed Donald Lang, without resistance or trouble of any kind. But the prisoner seemed unable to hear or speak. Denson thought he was faking. The truck driver denied this. He said the thing with Donny Lang was *point and he'd do it*. Denson pointed at the police car, and Lang moved towards it.

'Seemed a nice helpful kid,' said Denson. 'You get all kinds.'

At the ABLA Housing Project building the police knocked on the door of an apartment on the first floor and were admitted by Genettia Lang, Donald's sixteen-year-old sister. Julius Lang, a brother, aged 22, also lived there, but was at work. The three young people had lived in the apartment by themselves since the death of their mother three months before. The police treated Genettia considerately, but scared her, and she permitted them to look through the apartment. In a closet they found a light-coloured tan leather jacket which seemed to have blood spots on one arm and cuff, and a pair of trousers that also appeared to have been spattered. Genettia told the police these clothes belonged to Donald. They took the clothes and left. Genettia was very upset. Donald had never been in any trouble before. Julius wouldn't be home from work for a while, so she telephoned their older brother, William, who lived about two blocks away.

At Area 4 Headquarters on Maxwell Street, the Arrest Report officially identified the suspect as Donald Lang, AKA (also known as) 'The Dummy'.

'Upon arrival,' said the report, 'an attempt to communicate with Lang was made, with no apparent success.'

Denson was not so sure now that the prisoner was faking the blank inability to hear or speak. It was the first harassing appearance of a problem which was to create profound and indeed insurmountable legal difficulties. But the single-minded simplicity of basic police work advanced without pause.

Said Denson:

'He (Lang) took my pen from my pocket and drew a picture of a woman. Then he made a stabbing gesture towards my chest. I took it to mean he was telling me, "This is where I killed her." I took it to mean a confession.'

The official Police Report put it this way:

'Lang suddenly jumped to his feet and made motions towards Detective Denson as if attempting to portray some person stabbing another. His motions indicated a person driving a knife into the area of the heart of another, Lang using a pencil as the weapon. Lang then went on to act out a person tearing the clothing from another by gripping the clothing at the shoulders and making a downward motion.'

The Report continued:

'At this time it was decided to put Lang in a Squad car to drive to the scene.'

Another strategy:

'Due to the communication difficulty it was decided to stop at Lang's apartment at 1440 West 14th Street, and attempt to contact some member of his family who might aid in speaking to Lang. At the apartment the Detective located William F. Lang, male-Negro 29 years of age of 1625 West Washburne Avenue, brother of Donald. William Lang agreed to accompany the detectives with his brother to the murder scene.

'At the scene Donald Lang was let out of the car at the corner of Paulina Street and the east alley between Washburne and Roosevelt Road. Lang immediately proceeded to walk east in the alley, making various motions, and then into the gangway and to the doorway where the victim was found. Lang continued making various motions and proceeded to climb the stairs, at the foot of which the victim was found and at the top landing again enacted himself stabbing another person and then indicated that the person stabbed was pushed down the stairs. He continued to act out the part of a person running down the stairs and jumping over the supposed body at the bottom landing.'

The police were pleased, although William Lang injected a voice of doubt:

'Don't you see? He's trying to tell you that somebody, maybe several people, attacked him and the woman here!'

11

The police did not agree with that interpretation. Their momentum was irresistible to any logic of primitive sign language. They preferred to think that the prisoner had just signalled a reservation in the electric chair.

They took Donald Lang back to Area 4 Headquarters. He appeared to be no more disturbed than if he were merely a witness to a crime, not the suspect.

The police were slightly more disturbed. They could find no record for Donald Lang. It is difficult to accept that he grew up in the ghetto without one. But he was clean.

They showed Donald Lang the bloodstained jacket and trousers, known to be his personal property, and the police stated:

'When these pants were shown to Donald Lang, and the bloodstains were pointed out to him, he indicated a small scratch on his finger. He then was asked if he stabbed the victim. Donald then jumped up from a chair and went to a wastebasket which was in the interrogation room. He reached into this basket and pulled out a pocket knife. He was asked if he had put the knife into the basket. He indicated that he had done so. He then made pointing gestures in a stabbing motion.'

The police report concluded:

'Upon completion of this phase of the investigation the subject, Donald Lang was charged with murder, on recommendation of A.S.A. (Assistant State's Attorney) Parrish.' Lang was transported to the Central Detention to await hearing in court.

Donald Lang was taken to the Cook County Jail, and imprisoned for the first time in his life. The prison was a building not unlike most of the central business buildings of the city, a very large clump of sandstone with slots inside for each organism. Here, however, the slots were smaller and more sparsely furnished, and the doors were always locked.

Men sat or stood quietly in their cubicles, with no companionship possible. For the most part they were lower-paid workingmen of the city. A totally strange world to most individuals. But there, properly sealed away, unable to hear or speak, Donald Lang began to wait for justice.

On the morning of 24 November 1965, Donald, properly manacled, was taken under police escort to a hearing room of the Cook County Morgue for the official INQUEST ON THE BODY OF ERNESTINE WILLIAMS—FIRST & FINAL SESSION—BEFORE

THE CORONER OF COOK COUNTY. Deputy Coroners Clarence D. Myers and Anthony J. Sciaraffa conducted the proceedings. The jury of six men were sworn in at 11.30 a.m., with the record showing that they had previously been sworn in over the remains of Ernestine Williams at Cook County Morgue, the 13th day of November 1965.

Donald sat flanked by Police Officers. He looked about him and saw no familiar face, although his older brother William would appear later. He was without attorney, adviser or friend.

The Minutes of the Inquest were long, jumbled, surprisingly incomplete and confusing as to what would seem basic elements of the case.

Ernestine's brother A. J. Chatman once again testified covering essential matters already known, adding a few items. Ernestine was thirty-seven rather than thirty-eight, neither crippled nor deformed, height 5′ 4″, weight 126 lbs., father's name George Washington, social security number extant but unknown, two dependent children ages 17 and 19.

Det. Sgt. Louis Denson's testimony covered the facts of investigation already given in the Police Reports, with some of the confusions of details which were to characterize the overall official record of the Donald Lang case. Nothing intentional or malicious, but sheer carelessness, underscoring the curious situation in which the public relies on public records with little or no awareness of the patchy incompetence of the record-keepers.

It now appeared that 'Mr. Jackson' (Lee Jackson?) was taken to a room adjacent to the room where Donald was held in Area 4 Headquarters and there (or thereabouts) identified Donald as the person who left the Romeo Tavern with Ernestine somewhere between 11.00 and 11.15 p.m. on the night of November 11. Donald's employer was now given as Weber Trucking Lines instead of Harper Motor Van Lines, with Sid Harper unmentioned. Testimony now had it that Donald had been taken to the home of his brother, William F. Lang, Jr., at 1625 West Washburne, 'in order to see if he could communicate with him,' instead of to Apartment 105 at 1440 West 14th Street, as the police report had stated. According to the testimony of Mrs. Dorothy Hunter, Donald had approached another 'girl' in the Romeo that night, identified only as 'Mildred', and showed her money and pointed first to her 'privates' and then to the door and been refused by 'Mildred',

13

before connecting successfully with Ernestine in much the same observed way.

'May we have the next witness?' said one of the Deputy Coroners, not identified at this point in the record.

'Mary Jane Carter,' said Sergeant Denson.

'Who is that?' asked the Deputy Coroner.

'She had the coat,' said Sergeant Denson.

This appears to have done two things to the Deputy Coroner; it firstly confused him, and then brought on the immediate decision that Mary Jane Carter could have nothing important to say.

'All right, she has been identified as having been with her (Ernestine?),' said the Deputy Coroner. Mary Jane Carter was not called.

Mr. A. J. Chatman was the next witness called.

'Your name?' asked Deputy Coroner Clarence Myers.

'A. J. Chatman.'

'Your business or occupation?'

'I am on disability.'

'And you are the brother of the deceased?'

'Yes.'

'Let the record indicate that on the 12th day of November 1965, Mr. Chatman appeared before the morgue clerk and made positive identification of the deceased. Is that correct, Mr. Chatman?'

'Yes, it is.'

Lee Jackson was then called as a witness by Deputy Myers.

'Your name, sir?'

'Lee Jackson.'

'Are you employed, Mr. Jackson?'

'No. I am on the disability.'

'Disability?'

'Yes.'

'Now, Mr. Jackson, did you see Mrs. Williams in the Romeo Tavern the night of the 11th?'

'I seen her. She was playing some records.'

'Did she have anything to drink?'

'I didn't see her drinking, no sir.'

'Did you see anybody walk out of the tavern with Mrs. Williams?'

'Yes ... that guy right back there.'

'Are you indicating the accused, Donald Lang?'

'Yes.'

'And you saw Donald Lang with Mrs. Williams in the tavern?'

'Who?'

'Mrs. Williams,' the Deputy Coroner said, a faint note of irritation in his voice. 'Mrs. Williams, the woman that was found on the 12th.'

'You mean Ernestine?'

'Yes ... Ernestine.'

'Oh, sure. I knew her.'

'Did you see him with her?'

'No, I didn't see him with her.'

'Who *did* you see, then?'

'That guy right there.'

'That's who I'm talking about!'

'We call him The Dummy.'

'All right ... that is all, Mr. Jackson, thank you. Next witness.'

Dorothy Hunter was brought to the stand and sworn in.

'Your name?' asked Deputy Coroner Myers.

'Dorothy Hunter.'

'What is your business or occupation?'

'Disability.'

'You are on disability?'

'Yes.'

'What type of tavern is that?' Deputy Myers asked in exasperation. 'A tavern for disabled persons?'

'No, sir,' Mrs. Hunter said.

'There are more disabilities here than at 822 South Daman!'

Dorothy Hunter then testified that she had seen Ernestine Williams in the tavern. She had also seen Donald Lang in the tavern ...

'He was showing some money to my girl friend, Mildred, and pointing towards the door. She shook her head and said "No," and he bought her a beer and himself a beer. Ernestine was on the floor dancing. I left and went home and when I come back I seen him and Ernestine coming out of the tavern.'

Donald sat silently by, his handcuffs clanking when he stirred, as it was explained once again to a Deputy Coroner that he could neither hear, speak, write nor read.

'All right,' said one of the Deputy Coroners, not identified at this point, 'so the record will be clear, I will present a note to the defendant, and I will read what I am printing on here after I have him come up and get his Constitutional Rights. I understand that he doesn't understand anything and will not be able to testify, even if he wanted to, but I will, in the presence of the jurors, write a note to him and see his reactions and we will record it in the minutes.'

He then nodded to Donald whose reaction was not recorded.

'Let the record show,' said the Deputy Coroner, 'that I motioned to the defendant to have a seat before me.'

The record says nothing of Donald's movements at this time. It can be assumed that he was brought to his feet by a Police Officer and taken to the indicated seat in front of one of the Deputy Coroners.

'The note will be read by Deputy Myers,' said one of the Deputy Coroners, who could have been only Anthony J. Sciaraffa.

'Do you read, write or understand English?' Deputy Coroner Myers inquired of Donald.

'Show it to him,' said the DEPUTY, apparently A. J. Sciaraffa.

The record gives Donald's reaction as 'HE MUMBLED'.

'The only sound he makes,' said Sgt. Denson, apparently attempting to be helpful.

'Let the record show a shrug of shoulders,' said the DEPUTY, 'and a sound that is not understandable.'

The DEPUTY then inquired of Donald, 'Do you understand that?'

The record notes 'MORE MUMBLING'.

'Let the record indicate,' said the DEPUTY, 'there is no communication. All right, that is all.'

'WITNESS EXCUSED,' the record states, with the matter of his Rights, Constitutional and otherwise, unmentioned.

Sgt. Denson was recalled as a witness and Deputy Coroner Sciaraffa questioned him.

Q. Officer Denson, as the result of your investigation, is there a charge placed?

A. Yes, sir, there has been a charge of murder placed on Donald Lang, and he appeared in branch 43 on the 13th of November 1965, and the case was continued until the 30th of November 1965.

Q. To summarize then, Officer Denson, on the basis of the information you have received from people that were with Ernestine Williams on the 11th day of November 1965. In a

16

tavern located on the south-east corner of Paulina and Roosevelt and from your viewing of his actions when he was confined by Mr. Jackson, he got up from his chair, raised your shirt and took your pen from your pocket and made a thrusting motion towards the chest?

A. Yes.

Q. At that particular time and later, and walked and directed you to the area where the woman was found, that is the basis under which your charge is made?

A. Yes, plus the finding of the clothing in his home.

Q. Yes, which had apparent bloodstains?

A. Yes.

Q. Is that right?

A. Yes.

Denson was excused as a witness. William F. Lang, Jr. was found to be present, was called, sworn, admonished for being late, and questioned by Deputy Coroner Sciaraffa. After establishing William's identity and pertinence, the Deputy Coroner asked:

Q. We have learned from Officer Denson that your brother, Donald Lang, is a deaf mute?

A. Yes.

Q. Is that right?

A. Yes.

Q. He can't read or write, is that right?

A. Yes.

Q. And I have written a note to him (indicating) which reads, 'Do you read, write or understand English?' and he made a sound indicating he didn't understand. The investigation of the officer reveals on the basis of some evidence, and his actions, he had been charged with murder. Can you communicate with him in any way?

A. There is no way. He never had any type of formal education where you can communicate with him. He is illiterate, deaf and dumb and he knows no type of schooling. He was in school for a couple of months when he was small.

Q. You have been advised by the investigating officer the series of events that led up to his arrest?

A. Yes.

Q. Is there any way you can communicate with him to find out if the actions he had performed in the presence of Officer Denson, were or were not what they indicate?

A. Well, there was another officer with me at the time and I tried to communicate with him, and all he was saying was that he pointed to another individual out and said that was the man that did this.

Q. Who was the individual he had pointed out?

A. I don't know him. He was in the station at the time.

Q. Does Mr Donald Lang live alone or with somebody?

A. He is with my other brother. I have two other brothers and a sister.

Q. You are aware that there was some clothing found that had blood stains on them?

A. Yes.

Q. And they had been identified by witnesses on the 11th day of November 1965, when he was at the corner of Paulina and Roosevelt. The officers told you about that?

A. Yes.

Q. Anything you can add?

A. No, sir.

Deputy Coroner Sciaraffa started to dismiss William then asked if Deputy Coroner Myers had an opinion and a question.

DEPUTY MYERS: It is my opinion, deaf mutes are quick to anger. Is that the same with your brother?

MR. LANG: No, we have never had any trouble with him.

DEPUTY MYERS: Did he drink a lot?

MR. LANG: Well, this is, up to now, we don't know he had anything to drink. We found out then it was only beer, but he never drank in front of the family or any place.

DEPUTY MYERS: Would he display around home a violent temper?

MR. LANG: No.

DEPUTY MYERS: Did you know of him carrying a knife?

MR. LANG: Well, that is new. I talked to my brother about this and he said the only type of knife they know of was home now.

DEPUTY MYERS: What's that?

MR. LANG: It is home now, so, it is a pen knife, a pocketknife. It is home right now, and that's the only one they knew he had. Somebody said he had a knife with him but nobody seen it. That's about all.

DEPUTY MYERS: This knife is available for the officer to observe?

MR. LANG: Yes.

Deputy Myers: Was the brother raised by the father and mother?

Mr. Lang: Yes.

Deputy Myers: Or just the brothers and sister?

Mr. Lang: By a father and mother.

Deputy Myers: That is all.

The witness was excused by Deputy Coroner Sciaraffa who then asked if there was any further testimony to be presented. No response. Was there any reason why the Inquest should not be closed? No response. The Deputy Coroner then read the cause of death as signed by Dr Eugene Tapia, Coroner's Pathologist, on the 18th day of November 1965: 'It is my opinion, the said Ernestine Williams' death was due to stab wounds of aorta and lungs.'

The Deputy: You gentlemen of the jury have heard the witnesses, evidence and the testimony read in the record. You may now retire to a separate room and deliberate on your verdict, and when you have reached that verdict, you may call me and I will help you transcribe it in the proper legal form.

The Minutes state: 'Whereupon, the jury did then and there retire to a separate room and deliberated on their verdict, and having reached a verdict, returned shortly thereafter, and the following proceedings were had, to wit:

The Deputy: Have you gentlemen of the jury arrived at a verdict?

The Jurors: (in chorus) We have.

The Deputy: Is this your verdict, and so signed by you?

The Jurors: (in chorus) It is.

The Deputy: I will read the verdict, that is: The deceased, Ernestine Williams, came to her death on the 12th day of November, A.D. 1965, in the Cook County Hospital, dead on arrival, from and as a result of stab wounds of aorta and lungs; caused when the deceased was stabbed with a knife held in the hands of Donald Lang in an area-way and on a stairway in the rear of 1654 West Washburne in the City of Chicago, and was found on the 12th day of November 1965, at about 6 o'clock a.m. From the testimony presented, we the jury find this occurrence to have been murder and recommend that the said Donald Lang, now in police custody, be held to the Grand Jury of Cook County on the charge of murder until released by due process of the law.'

19

Donald was led back to his cell.

On 9 December 1965, he was manacled and taken before a Cook County Grand Jury and indicted for murder. He said nothing, and heard nothing insofar as could be determined.

On 15 December 1965, he was taken to a preliminary hearing in the courtroom of Alexander J. Napoli, presiding judge of Cook County's Criminal Court. There, a Public Defender was appointed as his lawyer.

What was the point of this heavy mechanism in either dealing with Donald Lang or helping him?

From the vast legal literature which was to be developed about him, the following fragment might be considered:

'He was seen in Cook County Jail on 17 January 1966. He was reasonably neat in appearance and again was unable to communicate. He stood with his back against the wall and forearms folded. Most of the time he watched the activities in the day-room and ignored the examiner. Frequently he would make grunts in a high-pitched tone and move his lips. He could understand signs such as the termination of the interview. Another inmate on the tier stated that he ate good and would take a shower when the shower was pointed out to him. *He is able to ape the behaviour of other inmates.* He is not aggressive and gets along well.

Diagnosis: Mutism. *He does not know the nature of the charges against him and is unable to co-operate with his counsel.*'

A central problem concerning Donald Lang had become more definite. Too simply stated, the difficulty was that the operative legal system, and the nation's fundamental law which the State's system was forced to recognize at certain key points, concerned themselves with human beings. They did not allow the substitution of aping for comprehension.

It was an embarrassment, but it was the law of the land.

And it became obvious that somewhere in the legal proceedings it would be helpful, although not required and certainly not guaranteed, for someone connected with the determination of justice to understand and communicate with Donald Lang. But who? What was the true nature of his case before the bar?

Donald Lang leaned against a wall of a day-room in the

Cook County Jail, his arms crossed over his chest, watching and waiting.

While the Public Defender had 200 cases on his assignment list —with no more than routine minutes for any of them—and the police were satisfied with their work and its limitations, there was some recognition of the law's responsibility to protect Donald as well as to prosecute him. It came from Judge Napoli, who was both fascinated and troubled as he studied the record to date—and he could not leave the quandary in his chambers when he went home.

What could be done with this young black? On the evidence, the charge of murder was justified. But where was the policeman, court officer or grand jury who could act out the charge and explain it to Donald Lang? They weren't as good at 'aping' as he was.

Oh, yes, they tried to write it out for him. When they handed him the slip of paper bearing the awesome words of a murder as foul as any ever committed in a Chicago alley, Donald signed the paper with a large X. It marked the spot of his illiteracy.

His reaction would have been the same to a charge of spitting on the sidewalk or a cheque for a million dollars.

It occurred to Judge Napoli in his ponderings that mere insanity would have been such a simplifying ingredient. The individual's right to trial could not be denied, and the court's necessity to recognize that right could not be avoided. It is called the due process of law and every man's right in the Constitutional society. Yet any basic ability to defend himself from any charges whatever was nowhere in view. Lang appeared from the record as a defendant who could not so much as acknowledge that he was on trial, not so much as complain that a lawyer's fee was too high.

In Judge Napoli's view, Donald Lang's predicament might well force upon jurisprudence a predicament greater than his own: Legal problems without precedent.

The Judge circulated highly intriguing and perhaps impossible questions among the bright young men of the State's Attorney's office. Where the attention of such busy and ambitious young men could be gained, they were not bright enough.

This did not surprise the Judge who found himself in the same dilemma. He had to proceed step by step, test by test, to see what sort of cloth had been woven as the fabric of the law to cloak even such as poor Donald Lang.

A jury would have to be empanelled to determine Donald Lang's physical competence to stand trial. Illinois law stated that a person who was physically incompetent to stand trial remained under court jurisdiction but did not specify what the court was to do with him. A procedural trap with an opening inward and no known way out.

Judge Napoli stared bleakly at the structure of the interrelated problems. The *law* could be so nicely flexible in the hands of a skilled Judge; the *procedural grid* was an iron cage.

One aspect of the situation was unwaveringly clear to Judge Napoli. Donald Lang would require the best defence obtainable. A routine Public Defender would add travesty to what could be legal helplessness, on both sides. A special man, an outstanding man was required. Somebody who could identify with the extra-legal problems of the defendant.

Judge Napoli wrote a short note to the only candidate who really qualified. It was to the only lawyer the judge knew who was totally deaf.

CHAPTER II

Lowell J. Myers was thirty-five years old when he first heard of Donald Lang. A tall, dark-haired man of muscular vitality and the look of a falcon on the hunt, Myers lived in a world almost as silent as Lang's. His hearing had been defective from birth and had faded completely at the age of twelve.

'Probably hereditary; both my father and mother were deaf-mutes. With me it was a gradual process, like a giant curtain gradually coming down and cutting off all sound. Going deaf is a dismal process. People open and close their mouths—but no sound comes out. Radios never work. There is no such thing as music. Dropping a pile of dishes makes no noise. There are no sirens or fire trucks. There are no horns on automobiles. There is no such thing as thunder. The world is filled with silence.'

But, unlike Donald Lang, Myers could speak. Hearing had been with him long enough to teach him use of the language. Deafness came upon him at a crucial stage of his development as a human being, and instructed him cruelly in the daily humiliations of the severely handicapped. He remembers the girls of his adolescence with particularly clear pain. They called him 'creepy'.

Profound hurt and helpless rage sometimes seized him. But he controlled it.

'I never cried until I was alone.'

Instead of seeking revenge and further humiliation, Myers turned the energy of his rage to the toughening process that bespeaks survival. Highly intelligent, an excellent student, his talents enlarged and strengthened as he used them in concentrated ways. He read and studied incessantly. He refused to allow his ambitions to be curtailed by his handicap, and instead tied them to the locomotion of aggressiveness. He learned lip-reading and sign language and became highly skilled in both.

Myers had the unwavering support and guidance of his parents. Without this, he believed, he would have been lost. His father was a printer, skilled and well-paid. There was sufficient money to provide a continuum of the special training he required. He lived in a comfortable and reassuring part of the city, a civilized neighbourhood. There was security and confidence to draw upon.

A kindly teacher told him that he would have to educate himself for a profession that did not rely upon verbal communication. Quite different longings had been developing in him, but at most times his practicality balanced aspiration.

'I went to Roosevelt University in Chicago and took a degree in business and accounting in 1951. I got a Masters Degree in Business Administration from the University of Chicago in 1952, became a Certified Public Accountant that same year.'

Figures not words. Books, ledgers, the endless complexity of financial documentation, not people.

Myers was quickly successful. Among other capabilities, he had the capacity to concentrate without distraction.

'The only problem was, I was bored stiff.'

The drama of life was too appealing. He wasn't ready to be locked off in the antiseptic cubicles of specialized financial management no matter how rewarding financially, and he had a growing suspicion that he never would be.

The partial exclusion from human relationships that his handicap had forced upon him, served, conversely, to increase the keenness of his interest and perception in what went on about him, along with an unusual awareness of the myriad and unremitting injustices practised by the more advantaged upon those less so. Those truly handicapped were obviously— to Myers—held at various levels of helplessness by personal circumstances beyond their power to alter or alleviate. He understood them in every nuance of their frustrations. But what would he do with them, for them or about them with the rows of numbers?

At times, when Myers roamed the streets of Chicago in his private silence, or sat at work on the problems of accountancy, he believed he could hear these disadvantaged people calling him: 'For Christ's sake, Lowell Myers, *do* something!'

In his own way, he was listening.

24

Myers' first thought was medicine. He could certainly help the disabled and the afflicted in that field—and he would meet and know people.

He would become a doctor! He would go back and fight his way through the required pre-medical education. He began applying to a series of medical schools—and they firmly forecast their rejection of him because of his handicap. What then? The law. He could study with the same zeal of his youth. He could read lips of judges and witnesses. He could, after all, still speak. And he could meet, deal with and help people in trouble.

'Impossible,' said well-meaning and knowledgeable friends.

Myers grinned bleakly and went to work. If he was deaf, all his friends seemed blind to the possibilities.

From 1952 to 1956, he worked as an accountant by day and studied law by night at the John Marshall Law School. He completed the work with honours, graduating number two in his class and receiving a Doctor of Jurisprudence Degree. That same year he was admitted to the Illinois Bar.

Practicality still guided aspiration. By that time, Myers was married and about to begin a family. He began to specialize in tax law and became a member of the Tax Department of the giant Sears Roebuck Company. But at night and in all spare hours, he practised the law of his choice. It was the law of the deaf and mute.

'I was, and still am, the *only* lawyer in the State of Illinois who knows the deaf-mute sign language and could make a speciality of practice with deaf-mute people. Many of their cases are unusual, fantastic, heart-breaking. For every deaf-mute person, there seem to be a hundred others to cheat or trick him by taking advantage of his handicap. And the deaf stumble into tragedy because they can't hear a warning while the mute can't explain why they are there. They get killed for not answering when someone demands an answer. And they get killed when they cannot hear danger approach or cry for help. The silent world is a hell of a place to live.'

Myers tried to make it better. For the deaf and mute, he even called up the courage to become a trial lawyer. He went into the courtrooms, fumbled, struggled, found his way. His older sister, Jean Myers Markin, took time from her husband and family to help him. She became his skilled assistant in courtrooms, his ears when he needed them. And she helped him as he struggled continually to improve his speech.

From a tentative beginning, he tried dozens and then hundreds of cases involving deaf persons and deaf-mutes. His skills grew, the respect of the legal profession increasing with his successes. Yet he remained a restless man, an essentially dissatisfied man. He had learned the law and its limitations in applying to deaf-mute individuals. Essentially, he decided, there was almost as much injustice as justice in it.

'What the hell, I thought, why not change the law if it didn't work. It's meant to serve mankind, not disenfranchise part of humanity.'

Myers personally forced through legislation that made the use of court interpreters mandatory for deaf-mutes in United States courts. He established a court order requiring that all deaf persons arrested in Illinois have an interpreter present when they were questioned. (When it was established—and ignored—he brought an action against the Superintendent of Chicago Police, and made it stick.)

Myers also fought for the passage of a state law allowing deaf persons to drive automobiles. When the legislation appeared likely to be bottled up in committee because of the 'disability' of the deaf, Myers investigated the committee members for disability. He discovered that four members were alcoholics, three myopic beyond the legal limit for car drivers, one helplessly crippled by arthritis—and all holding licences to drive. Myers wrote to each of these lawmakers of his findings —with carbon copies to their colleagues.

'The legislation was voted out of committee and approved at what I would guess to be 90 miles an hour.'

He didn't mind being regarded as a tough, intelligent, resourceful, sometimes ruthless young man. He figured he was. He'd had to be.

Whether they are motivated by handicap, greed, ambition or an astrological sign, there are men in the world who think they can do anything and everything—and do. Lowell Myers is one of them. With his daily job at Sears as a top specialist growing in quantity as well as quality of responsibility, the deaf-mute cases burgeoning into a heavy private practice, he decided to write a book for children. A very special book. It was to be used by deaf children when they went to school, and it explained the legal problems they might encounter. It has become a guide used by most deaf children in the United States.

'When it hasn't been distributed by an agency or acquired by a parent, the children themselves have somehow found out about it. Remarkable. I've gotten letters from deaf children asking for a copy—enclosing their lunch money to cover the costs.'

He also wrote a longer book entitled, *The Law and the Deaf*, to be used by lawyers and judges throughout the country. One large printing followed another.

Myers was, as he moved into his thirties, an extremely successful man in these endeavours. But it could not be measured in terms of financial wealth or even security. Many of his cases were assigned to him by the courts and were considered a 'public service' which meant that there was little likelihood of payment regardless of the amount of time and work required.

'Hard to turn down. If I didn't take them, who would?'

He seemed to be caught in an upward-rising spiral of *succès d'estime*—and personal poverty. And he was also fighting an unnerving personal battle for survival within the labyrinth of his alert mind: He was forgetting how words sounded, beginning to lose, as a consequence, his ability to articulate them.

What would happen when the memory failed completely? He would become incoherent, speak in meaningless sounds over which he had no control.

It was then that Judge Napoli wrote his note asking Myers to become involved in the problems of a black youth named Donald Lang. The boy was deaf, mute, illiterate, completely without financial resources and accused of murder.

Myers accepted immediately.

CHAPTER III

Before they met, Lowell Myers spent some time thinking about Donald Lang's thought processes and how they worked. They were thoughts of silence, of course—the boy had no words. Did Donald think in terms of images, movements or some symbology of gestures? Could he deal with abstract questions of right or wrong? There were a thousand questions like this for the attorney as he approached the first confrontation of client and counsel. It was ridiculous, Myers concluded, to even consider this first exploratory meeting as being in any way analogous or parallel to any such meeting Myers had ever had with a prospective client. For it all came down to a single bitter question:

What in the name of God's cruel pranks, did this vegetable Donald Lang know about what was happening to him or why?

Myers had asked that a trained person at the Cook County Jail communicate to the prisoner his function and purpose in the forthcoming visit. The request was ignored; the authorities were simply not equipped to deal with it. Myers had to go into the meeting cold. Explaining things to Donald Lang was his problem and his alone.

Then they faced one another across a narrow, grey, metal table, in a grey, windowless prison room. An armed guard hovered nearby. William Lang had told Myers that the family called the youth Donny. Myers repeated *Donny* several times in the clear flat penetrating voice that was there when he concentrated. There was no response. Donald Lang appeared to have no knowledge of lip-reading, which could mean he had no words at all. Myers recalls that he thought of the short, wide-eyed prisoner as a boy. He wondered how much experience had been deleted from the normal maturation process that would have given Lang the marks of his calendar years.

Myers held out his hand, Donald took it, tentatively, warily. Myers indicated that he could not hear, but did not try to explain that he wore a device in one ear that measured the vibrating of his own sounds, and thus provided a physical indication through vibrations that he was talking too loudly or softly. ('Without the vibes, I could be yelling and not know it.') Now it became a device to involve Donald.

Myers touched the device, gesturing that he could not hear. Lang was interested. Myers voiced a few exaggerated word enunciations, establishing that these meant nothing to Lang.

Myers had to start from scratch, from behind scratch. Lang heard absolutely nothing. The facial movements of even strongly exaggerated speech were meaningless to him. The grunts and moans in Donald's throat could form nothing approaching the shape of a single word.

Myers wrote something on his pad, large clear lettering. Donald stared at it. Lowell handed him the pen. Donald hesitated. Lowell pointed with his forefinger, duplicating the writing movements. With the pen Donald imitated the same writing, remarkably skilful in this. Meaningless except for the skill and alertness required. But at least Myers knew alertness was there and that the hands were unusually capable. Point-and-do seemed the limit. There was no bridge of real communication that Myers might cross to seek the truth of what had happened on 11 to 12 November, to seek the truth of Donald Lang.

Myers held up the ballpoint pen. Donald stared at it. Myers took apart the fairly complicated writing instrument, scattering the pieces out on the table, spring, ink cartridge, point and casing. He indicated the pieces and then made a gathering gesture with his fingers. Lang's eyes turned away, as if failing to comprehend the problem, or rejecting it. But Myers simply sat there, insisting with his presence. He had noted a slight change of expression in the boy's eyes. He repeated his gesture. Lang looked again at the pieces of the pen.

Almost casually, lightly, one powerful workman's hand touched one part of the pen. Then the fingers became swift and skilful. They put the pen back together considerably more quickly than Myers could have done.

Myers left the table. The guard moved towards it. Myers gestured that he was returning immediately. Without looking back, he could feel Lang's eyes following him with his other senses and the all-inclusive peripheral vision that is an instrument of survival in the world of the deaf. Myers brought back a container of coffee and put it on the table between them.

He spent over an hour teaching Donald the sign language for coffee. Alertness was there, but the habits evolved from birth remained rigid, irremovable now. Had no one, ever, tried to teach this boy, to help him? Apparently not. Myers 'asked' Donald if he wanted the cup of coffee, repeating this again and again. Donald watched him blankly, then turned his eyes away. Myers continued to repeat the question, knowing that Lang was aware.

Suddenly the boy uttered a high wailing cry, his throat shuddering, the guard jumping towards them. Myers could not hear it, of course, but he saw the throat muscles constrict.

'What the hell's wrong?' the guard demanded.

Lowell, who had been peripherally watching the guard, understood the man's words well enough. Myers reassured the guard that it was all right. Then he went back to the question for Lang about the cup of coffee. And Donald finally shook his head. Myers also screamed himself. The boy was communicating. He was saying 'No'—he didn't want the coffee, didn't understand or didn't want to be bothered. Whatever, it was a breakthrough!

And before he left the jail that day, Myers knew what he or any teacher was up against: It would take years, perhaps between five and ten years of intensive training to equip Donald Lang with sufficient sign language that would enable him to discuss his possible role in the murder of Ernestine Williams and prepare for the attack of the prosecution. Years and years. And the court had given them fifteen days. Myers thought of the young State's attorneys in their beehive of offices on the second floor of the WPA-Gothic Criminal Courts Building, so confident that they were going to put Donald Lang away as a killer. A smooth and simple case in which the defence was a cardboard castle.

He put away his pen, finished the cold coffee and dropped the carton into a wastebasket. Two devices of brief, blurred, meaningless communication. Donald watched the simple actions. He waited. They both waited. Myers wondered how much Donald felt of the aching frustration that was inside him.

Donald's eyes moved about the room, but Myers knew they

were watching him. The eyes came back and for a moment looked hard and clear into his own. He couldn't stand the raw, primitive demand in the liquid brown eyes for a justification of their presence together in this steel cage, in this human prison of silence. Shaken to the foundation of all his security and peace, Myers could only get up and go.

Jean Myers Markin went to her brother's home to make coffee —one of the few things he did badly—and to sit with him in the den-library where he worked. Just the two of them. He was grateful to have her there. Eight years older, always thoughtful, her hearing and speech completely normal, this sister had always been an anchor and refuge for Lowell Myers. And she was also the skilled assistant he required in courtrooms and related situations. She was waiting patiently now, while he went over his notes on Donald Lang.

For many years, they had communicated with total clarity through his skilled lip-reading of her subtly exaggerated enunciations and her instant comprehension of any speech pattern he might follow. They were tuned to each other.

In recent years, however, there had been a blurring of these mutual skills on his part, still slight but frightening to him. Indications of greater difficulties to come. He was losing the battle to the relentless rule that all function incapable of improvement will retrograde. Gradually his memory of words and speech patterns became dimmer, was fading and he was losing his ability to speak understandably.

'I have begun retreating,' he had said to Jean, his voice too strong under the emotional pressure.

Mrs. Markin understood. She was filled with admiration for the sheer unremitting power of character and will that enabled her brother to force back the clamping walls of his disability and to grasp such remarkable achievements. And she knew the depth of his personal and professional pride. Now she could foresee the darker and narrower world into which the 'retreating' would force Myers with the anguish and loss this would involve.

Myers had already told her something of the Donald Lang case. She had some understanding of what would be its unusual difficulties and pressures. She feared the immensity of the test it would be for him. She regretted, for once, that Myers' obsession with justice for the handicapped had attached itself to this young, black man accused of murder, and yet she was deeply proud of his response to the challenge.

'What I will have to do,' he was telling her, 'is learn everything possible about Donald Lang, everything in his life.'

'Won't that be terribly difficult. He can't help you ... and his family ... people of that kind ...'

'What kind? They're human.'

'So much time has passed ...'

'Only nineteen years,' said Lowell wryly. 'You'll have to help me.'

She nodded. A pledge of her own. She had never failed to help Myers in matters of importance to him.

Following the death of their deaf-mute father, she had taken Myers and their deaf-mute mother into her home. Lowell was totally deaf and in the most difficult period of struggle to lay the foundations for a satisfactory life. He was in high school, fighting the handicaps in both academic and social areas. He had begun 'running wild' as he sought ways to somehow relieve the agonizing frustration of being the constant outsider, the handicapped alien who could only achieve a citizenship of notoriety, of the 'gang'.

The barriers between Myers and his mother, of course, were higher, more forbidding than most because of her handicap. If anyone was to undertake the job of bringing him under control it had to be his sister, Mrs. Markin. She undertook it without reservation.

Later, when Myers had left Mrs. Markin's home for a marriage of his own (a marriage that was never an easy one, never geared to work well), their alliance remained strong. This phase of his life had intersected his enormous efforts to gain his education in law and establish the beginning of his career as a lawyer. They had two children—Linda and Benjamin—but the marriage ended in divorce, and Mrs. Myers died shortly afterwards.

The children became Myers' total responsibility—with Mrs. Markin's helpful assistance. The children were asleep as Myers and his sister talked.

'Who is Donald Lang, what's the truth about him?' he was asking himself. 'He watches me, the way I watch him, the way we watch everybody. He keeps looking back and all around him, like me. He has to keep the world in focus with only his eyes. What's his world really like?'

Where do you commence the excavation? Society had almost, but not quite, buried Donald Lang. There had to be a hole somewhere.

Lang was a day labourer and at the time of the murder, had been so for years. His place of work was the starting-point.

Lowell Myers knew Chicago—times and places.

The markets and warehouses of Chicago are concentrated in a four-block area running along 15th Street, west of Morgan. One side is the skyline of the buildings of the ABLA Housing Projects, where Donald lived through nearly all of his growing-up years. This is where Myers began his search and began to find remnants of Donald Lang's life.

Mario Pullano, a loading boss on the docks. A tall and big man, powerfully muscular in his fifties after decades of labour. A friend of Donald Lang.

'He used to wander over from the Projects every day, when he was about ten years old. First thing you know he was helping people on the trucks and the guys give him a buck or two. We'd take him along to Tony's (the Market Top, favourite eating place for the workmen) and he got so he'd follow me around like a shadow. I really got to like the kid. We all did. Deaf an' dumb but so bright an' good-hearted. Some 'a the guys would call him "The Dummy" but they was never mean about it. He was like one of us. We'd never make fun of him. We'd see nobody'd horse him around.'

Tony Gosentino, owner of the Market Top bar and grill, and the workers hanging around there, were friends of Donald Lang. They had hard workingman's questions. Did the whore try to trick-hustle him? Did she try to roll him for his wallet? Did she have somebody jump him when he was in the saddle? They were questions the police hadn't answered. Said Tony Gosentino:

'The Dummy never looked for trouble. I remember one day he was here drinking a beer and a hillbilly and a coloured guy came in—strangers. They started getting drunk and started swinging at each other. The Dummy went over and picked up the guy who was doing most of the swinging and carried him out the door. He didn't like to have people fighting around him.

'Strong? Jesus, yes. Not big, but a powerhouse. Just for fun, he'd lift Mario Pullano up over his head, and Mario must go

33

around two-fifty. It was like the way he was about working, he loved it, it was *fun* for him. All the guys really liked him and respected him about that. He was something special.'

One of the big workmen recalled that Donald was competitive about his work.

'He'd hustle trailers just like me. Couple of times he thought he'd got the job ahead of me. So he'd come up and step on my toes and make me quit. Even as a kid, he could do a man's work. He picked up a hundred-pound bag of beans, just like that.'

Donald could make eight to fifteen dollars a load and averaged about ninety a week.

'He'd sometimes ask me to hold his money for him,' said Mario Pullano. 'I'd give him maybe ten dollars, but first thing on Monday he'd come and ask for his money. He was sharp about money but always fair and honest. I taught him how to tell the right change for things. Teach him once and he'd never forget. He memorized the shape of the coins.

'He couldn't tell time, but we'd point at numbers and he'd come back at the right time. Sometimes I'd be waiting for a trailer to pull in, I'd have some time so I'd write his name for him. He'd try but he'd mix it up and reverse the letters. Then he'd get that disgusted look on his face and throw it away. His handicap was just too much for him that way. It would really tear you up inside, to see how hard he'd try. I guess nobody ever tried to help him, that way, when he was little. Goddamned shame, so lousy unfair to the kid.

'But what I'm trying to say, he worked so damned hard with what he had and made a life for himself. Most of the time you could just show him something and he'd understand. He'd get that expression, "Oh yeah, sure." He really wanted to drive the truck and I had to keep explaining why he couldn't get a licence. But he was an expert on the lift-truck, the jeep. He could really wheel it around. He would pat it, start it up, then bend over as if he was listening to it. He could take the thing apart, too, and put it back together again.

'He used to get here at 7.30 in the morning from the time he was a kid. We'd find him here very neat with his clothes in a duffle bag. He'd fill up the fork-lift with gas and go get coffee for us. It was like he had a kind of joy in his work. Something special. It felt good just to be with him.

'It was like he had a special kind of pride in things around here. Some of those coloured kids from the Projects, they'd come over here and try to rip open the bags. But he'd watch out for them, even when he was little. He'd never touch those kids but he'd chase 'em off. He was *kind* about everything. There was a dog wandered in here, going to have pups. He took care of her, fed her, used to give her baths in the back.

'What I'm trying to say is that Donald wasn't all shut off an' *dumb*, you know, without feeling an' ways of seeing things. He was no *dummy* that way. He was so damned aware of things other people hardly noticed, like the weather an' the look of things ... an' helping people without being asked to ...'

Donald Lang had a world and it was anchored in the companionship and respect of workingmen, a male world. What about girls and women? He was accused of killing a woman. Donald's older brother William was some help here, in the beginning of the investigation. But clearer indication first appeared at the work-place. There were a few office girls there to handle the vouchers and records. One of these, a small, dark girl of Italian lineage with a beehive hairdo:

'Oh, sure, I remember him. He was sweet. He used to kind of like me, I think, and we'd sort of kid around. Whenever I'd bring my dog to work, he'd want to take it for a walk. He was nice. But he was awful shy, too, kept his distance sort of, like he was maybe scared of girls a little.'

But there were also women who did not scare Donald. The hookers arrived at the market in the late afternoon. They hustled the truckers after the loads were finished. Black girls, who came sauntering in with the afternoon sun.

Said Mario Pullano:

'The hustlers make out in the cabs of the trucks. I fixed Donald up a few times, you know, as soon as he was old enough. With his handicap, what was he going to do with other kinds of girls? I'd fix him up for five dollars, that's what these hustlers charge. He'd let me know if he wanted one— you know, make gestures—and I'd make a deal for him. Why not? He's just like anybody else.'

Myers had a clearer picture of the puzzle he was attempting to put together. But he needed more pieces. Perhaps they were in his home life, his childhood.

35

Donald had learned a key lesson early in life, according to his older brother William. There was a time when he was thirteen or fourteen, playing with a younger girl, and they began exploring each other's bodies. Like a lot of other children, they were discovered by adults who have long since suppressed the memory of their own childhood explorations.

'Or maybe,' observed William Lang, 'a child who couldn't hear or speak wasn't supposed to have such feelings or do such things.'

'There was a great fuss. The mother of the girl called the police and they took note of it. Donald's mother had him examined by a psychiatrist and he took note of it. But it began and ended in a flurry of minor embarrassment.

'He couldn't hear it,' William Lang adds, 'but all that jumping up and down and finger waving shook him up. He stayed away from girls—until they showed him the ones down at the loading dock.'

When Myers first ventured into the ghetto in search of clues to the mystery of Donald Lang, he encountered some problems of his own. He was white and nosey; the community was black and hostile.

'Donald's brother, William, was worried about me,' Myers has recalled. 'He felt it just wasn't safe—and it wasn't. William is the leader of a social-religious group of black Jews, and from that group he formed a kind of Praetorian guard to accompany us wherever we went.'

That meant going from door to door.

'Doors that were usually slammed with a snarl of a huge watchdog. Everybody in the ghetto has a big, vicious dog. We ended up back on the sidewalk.'

But the word got around that Myers was asking about the deaf-mute youth in jail, that Myers was trying to help.

'They came out and talked then,' and Myers learned that Lang had a good and special reputation in the neighbourhood. He had gotten along unusually well with nearly everyone, particularly the older people, whom he seemed to want to help.

The tight circle of Donald Lang's personal geography became more meaningful as Lowell Myers traversed it. The oddly spectacular gingerbread house of William Lang, Jr. was only two

36

blocks from the project building where Donald had lived and the murder took place only two blocks from this house.

The ABLA Housing Project intrigued Lowell, its history and what he considered the foolishness of placing it here, instead of channelling all that money into a more neighbourhood sort of redevelopment deeper in the South Side. The blacks were more in charge of their own lives on the South Side and in all basic ways life was more orderly there. When Martin Luther King was assassinated, the black leaders of the South Side told the police to stay out and they would see that things didn't get out of hand. Things didn't. It was the Near West Side that rioted and burned.

William Lang, nine years older than Donald Lang, and also known as Levi Yisrael, said at this time that perhaps the secret of Donald's life died with their mother, Julia.

'It was like we all had a piece of Donny and none of us had him all, except for our mother, and it's too late for that.

'She didn't have the name Lang legally. My father never married her, and then he left her and married a younger woman. Not a bad man, worked in steel for Youngstown Sheet and Tube mostly, still works when he's up to it. Always drank quite a lot. Now with my mother, with Julia Lang and Donny, there was this real closeness, like they were connected. Too bad she isn't here to tell you.'

Myers learned little from the father, William Lang, Sr., who said that Donald was not a boy who would do anything like kill somebody, always took care of himself, and never got into trouble.

'If Donny gets out of this trouble someway,' he added, 'it might be all right for him to come back an' live with us here.'

Other meetings, with Donald's brother Julius and younger sister Genettia with whom he was living at the time of the murder, evoked the gentle but strong presence.

'We never could understand what it was caused his deafness,' Julius said. 'Dropping from the cradle, we think. Momma used to think that, and she would hold him and hold him, like he was a part of her. The best time for Donny was when he was going to the Parkman School down on the South Side, when he was just a bitty boy, hardly more than a baby. He could say a couple of words then. Momma and his own name. Most it was calling out to her. "Momma," he would say and just keep saying it over and over.

'Yes, he had those couple of words then and Momma kept hoping he would get more. She *knew* he could get more. But they wouldn't keep him at the Parkman School, they wouldn't keep him anywhere although Momma would beg them.'

Donald Lang's mother died three months before the murder of Ernestine Williams. The significance of Mrs Lang's death, the impact on Donald's attitudes, have gone unmeasured. The death of a parent is always a serious displacement to the security structure of the child. But most children, at least those in their late teens, have been conditioned to the life-death cycle by experience, training and education. Was Donald prepared in any way or, in fact, could he have been?

And who could Myers ask about it other than his family? They had no answers.

'Maybe nothing would have happened to Donny,' said Genettia, 'Maybe Donny would've stayed home more and not got into trouble if Momma was alive. He used to like to stay home with Momma, but then he was different. Like her dying changed him, like something went out of him.'

Donald's personal geography did not so much widen as take one deep dip southward, into the famed and often defamed black ghetto of Chicago's South Side, Donald's homeland, the place of his birth, 5702 Wabash.

The house was dingy and battered and tattered. It had been condemned long ago. But it was a house, a family-type house, a few trees, a feeling of neighbourhood, a sense of community.

'I wasn't here when they had to move to the Projects,' said William. 'I was off in the Air Force. This was where Donny lived his first eight years or so. This was home to him.'

William gave Donald's birth date as 15 January 1945. Lowell Myers made special note of that date and later verified it against Donald's birth certificate. Police records incorrectly listed Donald's age as nineteen at the time of his arrest, a year younger than he actually was.

The birth was normal, although Julia Lang had been ill during the pregnancy.

The baby was breast and bottle fed alternately. Julia didn't like the bottle, but her milk didn't seem to be good or ample enough.

At approximately five weeks of age, while Donald was sleeping in his home-made crib, the bottom fell out of it, and he crashed to the floor. American doctors do not make home calls

in the Chicago slums, any more than they do in better neigh-
bourhoods. But they are, in the ghetto at least, so rare for any
emergency that it is understandable, if not forgivable, that no
examination was made of the baby after the accident.

As time passed, Julia noticed that her baby did not seem to
respond to noises around him the way he should. But he was
a very quiet boy, anyway, and he was still so small.

She weaned him at around ten months of age. He began
walking at eleven months. She had some trouble toilet training
him, more than with the other children. He remained a very
quiet baby, and Julia's worries about him were growing. She
could no longer deny that he just didn't seem to hear things
the way he should. She took him to a doctor who confirmed
her fears, saying that Donald's deafness was the result of a
'nerve deficiency' and could not be treated or helped in any
way. It was difficult for her to read the doctor's careless scrawl
but she deciphered the key words, and they stayed with her
forever.

'Nerve deficiency—hopeless.'

The man was a real doctor and he looked and sounded very
intelligent and absolutely sure about everything. He had told
her and written down that nothing could ever be done for
her baby to make him hear. But Mrs. Lang was also aware
that doctors never had much time for the ghetto black who had
limited resources for special care. She took the baby home and
continued to wonder how she could find out what the words
really meant.

Mrs. Lang began making the rounds of city, county and state
agencies that might provide either the answers—or the assistance to buy the answers in the open market of medicine. This
was an exercise in deafness, too, for if they heard, the agencies
were incapable of responding. It was two years before a func-
tionary in one of these agencies suggested the Parkman Deaf-
Oral School on 51st Street in the same Englewood District of
the South Side where she lived. She took Donald there. He was
two-and-a-half years old and he stayed only a few weeks.

The school said he had not been adequately toilet trained,
as members of the family now recall the disappointment, and
suggested that Donald be examined for retardation, resulting
from possible brain damage.

This was the beginning and the end of Donald Lang's formal
training. He stayed at home, close to his mother and proceeded

to grow up. His conversation consisted of squeaky little sounds when he was happy or hurt. He learned to laugh in a high squeal and would make different wailing sounds when he was upset. He could—and would—do what he was shown to do, which is neither autistic nor damaged behaviour.

Mrs. Lang hoped that Donald would be able to attend public school when he turned six. When the day came, she enrolled him—and explained all the things that Donald could do as well as his limitations. She was hardly home again when the school called and insisted that Donald be removed. There was no way the system could be adapted to his special needs.

Julia Lang was left with five children when William Lang, Sr. left the household and established another.

She kept the children together by working, obtaining some public assistance. She also persisted with incredible determination to seek help for Donald.

The following is a fragment from a report dated 25 January 1955 by one Morris Ellman to the 'Medical Social Unit, Division of Crippled Children, Chicago Regional Office'.

'Mr. Lang, at present, is believed to be married and resides with his wife and family at 2920 South State Street. He reportedly visits Julia Lang and the family occasionally but does not contribute towards their support. Mrs. Julia Lang has five children and works to support them as her health will allow. The eldest son enlisted in the Air Force last month and is now in California. The other children, with the exception of Donald are in school ... Mrs. Lang and her children are the sole occupants of a six-room dwelling space at 5702 South Wabash which, while in need of extensive repairs, is modestly furnished and apparently adequate for the needs of the family ... Donald, the second youngest child, had been a deaf-mute since birth. He is a rather attractive, outgoing child, and seemingly very independent, in spite of his handicap. When he wants to gain attention, he either gestures or draws the objects he wants ... In 1949, Mrs. Lang accompanied Donald to attend a conference for pre-school deaf children in Jacksonville, Illinois. Since that time she has apparently become more cognizant of the problem her son must confront through the literature and pamphlet material sent to her by the Chicago Hearing Society. Mrs. Lang also attends any meeting arranged by the hearing faculty, and in June of last year arranged to go to a meeting scheduled at that time ... Mrs. Lang has been very disconcerted over the fact that Donald has been excluded from school. She has expressed willingness to abide by any decision made which is for his welfare ... We would also like to advise that in the past Mrs. Lang always took Donald to the clinic whenever appointments were scheduled, and only on one occasion did she permit her eldest son to take him. We hope that this information will be helpful.'

File and forget. No agency, public or private, would do anything for Donald Lang.

In 1955, at the urging of the Welfare supervisors, Mrs. Lang moved her family from the six-room house on Wabash Avenue into a two-bedroom apartment on the ground floor of a fifteen-story, yellow brick building in the ABLA Housing Project. The building, one of six identical structures that formed the project, was situated on 14th Street on the Near West Side, three blocks from the South Water Market that would play such a major role in Donald Lang's development. Mrs. Dolly Gill, who had lived in the same building as the Langs, remembered Donald well.

'He was always playful, always doing joke things like knock on my door and then hide, pretending nobody was there. He'd come up and borrow my kids' bicycle because he never had one of his own. They never minded lending it to him because he was always careful and brought it back. He even shined it up and put air in the tyres. He loved to take it apart and grease it.'

Life in the vertical ghetto of the project was raw and sometimes brutal, but Donald survived. He became street-wise and well attuned to his environment.

'Donny saved the life of my boy Kenneth,' Mrs. Gill recalled. 'Kenneth was four years old and Donny was maybe ten. He came running up to me and made those o-o-o-o- sounds he made, and grabbed my hand until I'd come with him. When I got downstairs, a man in the hallway had my Kenneth bent over with his pants down and he was—you know—doing things to him with a stick. Well, the man ran off when he saw me. Two weeks later, he raped a little girl in the hall and stuck her with an ice-pick.'

The ABLA Housing Project stands in the city's worst crime

area, a concrete and brick jungle that the police from Maxwell Street (Area 4 Homicide) patrol in careful twos. Life is cheap, with an average of two hundred and fifty murders a year, the highest homicide rate in Chicago's six police areas. Donald Lang grew to young manhood in this district. He learned to play basketball on the project's crowded playground and to swim at the local YMCA, but his silence kept him apart from most of the other kids. He was a loner in a world of tightly knit gangs. Sometimes the gangs accepted him and sometimes they didn't.

'He'd catch hell on the streets,' his brother Julius said. 'But you couldn't keep him in. None of us could stay with him all the time. He couldn't get in school and he used to run away all the time. It used to worry my mother, and she'd worry us. He'd be gone a week maybe, or a week-end. We never knew where he went because he couldn't write us or call us. When the carnival came around, he'd go off with them, but he always came back. He'd be real dirty, like maybe he'd been working for them. But we never did know for sure.'

The oldest brother, William Lang, had become a karate expert in the Air Force and had taught the art while stationed in Tokyo. After leaving the service, he lived two blocks from the family and saw Donald nearly every day.

'I didn't want to teach him karate,' William said. 'That's a martial art and I wasn't sure Donny could control himself with it. Donny, by nature, wasn't violent. If you pushed him in a corner, he would fight, but after that he would cry. We all wanted to fight his battles, but I said we couldn't because he had to learn. Once Donny was set upon by two guys with a lead pipe. I was watching until they started to use that pipe and then I stepped in. Donny had offered them money, but they jumped him anyway. I took the pipe away from them and made Donny fight them one at a time so he could learn to protect himself. Kids would get on him, not because they disliked him, but because they couldn't understand him. He was different.'

Under his adopted name of Levi Yisrael, William Lang is the leader ('Kohn') of the B'nai Zaken Temple, the meeting place of the 'Hebrew Israelites', located a half block from the Romeo Tavern where Donald Lang had picked up Ernestine Williams. Levi and the men in his congregation wear dashikis, Gandhi-like caps, and .38s. 'We are peaceful,' he said, 'but when our women

42

are being raped coming to the temple, we must take action.' Levi says he is going to lead his people to Ghana in the next ten years. Meantime, the congregation is under constant threat. The temple is now called 'The Camp', and classes in self-defence have been added to the courses in reading and languages. Levi says his association with the Black Hebrew movement grew out of his mother's interest in it. He wishes he had followed it when he was growing up, but 'I was too busy ripping and running'.

Of his brother Donald, Levi Yisrael says, 'In this part of town Donny is a sitting duck.' Levi speculates that Donald may have been set upon by people who were out to get him (Levi). Levi's home has a constant guard around it. Even so, it has been bombed twice.

Lowell Myers gathered these bits and scraps and put together a montage that represented Donald Lang. It was a sketchy portrait, but there appeared to be an innate quickness and intelligence about him, a potential that had been locked away in the terrible silence of his life. Lowell Myers thought of his own childhood experiences and treatment. The contrast appalled him.

CHAPTER IV

On 20 January 1966, Lowell Myers, attorney-at-law, appeared in court with his new client for the first time. The purpose of the hearing was to determine Donald Lang's competency to stand trial on the charge of murder.

Ned D. Hosford, a court reporter of the Circuit Court of Cook County, began the transcript of the hearing while the jury filed silently into the box. He wrote, in meticulous shorthand—

DONALD LANG, Petitioner VS THE PEOPLE OF THE STATE OF ILLINOIS, Respondent. Indictment No. 65-3421. Charge: Murder. COMPETENCY HEARING. Be it remembered that on the 20th day of January, A.D. 1966, before the Honourable ALEXANDER J. NAPOLI, Presiding Judge of said court, this cause came on for hearing upon the petition heretofore filed. APPEARANCES: MR. LOWELL J. MYERS, Court appointed counsel, Appeared for the Petitioner; HON. DANIEL P. WARD, State's Attorney of Cook County, By Mr. Charles Barish and Mr. Truman Larrey, Assistant State's Attorneys, Appeared for the Respondent.

Lowell Myers took his seat at a table facing the jury box. Donald Lang sat beside him, slouched in his chair, bored and uncomprehending. There was no way that the importance of what was about to take place could be communicated to him. He stared at the jury members and they stared back. Lowell Myers kept his eyes on the court clerk, waiting for the man's lips to move.

'Donald Lang,' the clerk intoned.

Lowell Myers rose to his feet and faced the bench. 'Your Honour,' he said, 'I would like to have leave of court to file my petition for the hearing by the jury on the question of whether or not the defendant is physically competent to stand trial.'

Judge Napoli nodded his assent. 'All right. We'll file the petition. We have twelve jurors in the box. Are they acceptable to you?'

They were acceptable to Myers and to Truman Larrey, the State's Attorney. There was no point in prolonging the proceedings by questioning the panel. These twelve Chicago citizens would be as impartial as any others. Judge Napoli asked them to rise and they were sworn in. Myers waited until they were seated and then he addressed them, facing them squarely, a tall, athletic looking man. There was nothing in his manner to suggest that he was as deaf as his client.

'Ladies and gentlemen of the jury, you are here for the purpose of determining whether or not Donald Lang is physically capable of standing trial. That is the only purpose of this hearing. I will prove to you that Donald Lang is a deaf-mute and he has been a deaf-mute from birth, I believe. He cannot speak and he cannot hear and he cannot read or write and he cannot read lips and he doesn't know sign language. It is impossible for anyone in the world to communicate with him, and therefore, he cannot stand trial.'

Truman Larrey then stood to make the opening statement for the State. He clarified the issue for the jury. The State did not deny that the defendant was a deaf-mute. The jury was simply to determine, on the basis of the evidence that would shortly be submitted to it, whether or not Donald Lang was competent or incompetent to stand trial for the charge pending against him. He did not specify what that charge was.

'If he is found competent he would stand trial,' the young prosecutor said. 'If he is found incompetent, he would not stand trial, but would be sent away to a State hospital for treatment.'

Myers objected to that remark. The law did not necessarily state that a man found physically incompetent to stand trial be sent anywhere, but Judge Napoli brushed aside the objection.

'The court will decide where he will be sent at the proper time.'

The words ... *sent away to a State hospital for treatment* ...
remained in the record.

Myers called himself as the first witness. He told the jury of his
frustrating experiences in trying to communicate with his
client, of his efforts to break through to him by using the
accepted tools of the deaf—sign language, lip reading, pointing and drawing pictures of simple objects. Only through the
use of pictures had he been able to make any headway.

'I was able to draw a picture of his home,' Myers said, 'and
it took me about a half-hour to try and make him understand
that I was asking him if he wanted to go home. And after
about a half-hour I think he started to get the idea and nodded
yes. I was able to get two or three ideas across to him that
way but that was the maximum of what I was able to do with
him.

'Now, on the basis of my experience with deaf-mute people,
it is my opinion that this man is a true deaf-mute person. He
has never been educated in any system of communication
and it is my belief that there is no one in the world who can
communicate with him sufficiently to make him understand a
criminal indictment, a criminal trial, and have him co-operate
and communicate with his lawyer. I do not believe it can be
done.'

The jury gazed at Donald Lang and Donald Lang gazed back.

'Put the doctor on the stand,' Judge Napoli said. 'Swear in
Doctor Haines.'

William H. Haines, M.D., was a man with impeccable credentials. A graduate of the University of Minnesota Medical School
in 1932, Dr. Haines had served on the staff of the Psychiatric
Institute of the University of Illinois, at the Mayo Clinic and
at Bellevue Hospital in New York City. A specialist in nervous
and mental diseases, he was currently director of the Behaviour
Clinic, Criminal Court of Cook County. He had been brought
into the case by order of Judge Napoli and had made his first
examination of Donald Lang on 3 January 1966, and again on
17 January. He was to be Lowell Myers' sole witness at the
hearing.

'Did you ever attempt to examine the defendant?' Myers
asked.

46

Dr. Haines nodded. 'I did.'

'Were you able to communicate with him?'

'I was not.'

'What is your diagnosis on his case?'

'Mutism.'

'I have no further questions, your Honour.'

Myers sat down and Truman Larrey cross-examined for the State.

'As a result of your examination of the defendant, Doctor Haines, would you classify the defendant as competent or incompetent?'

'I would classify him as incompetent.'

'And as a result of your examination of the defendant, do you have an opinion as to whether he knows the nature of the charge against him?'

'I have.'

'And what is that opinion, doctor?'

'That he does not know the nature of the charge pending against him.'

'And based upon your examination of this defendant, do you have any opinion as to whether he can co-operate with counsel?'

'I have.'

'And what is that opinion?'

'That he is unable to co-operate with his counsel.'

There were no further questions and Dr. Haines was dismissed. The State had no evidence to submit in opposition to the testimony given. The procedure had been a mere formality between the officers of the Court. After retiring to chambers with Dr. Haines, Lowell Myers and the two State's Attorneys, Judge Napoli returned to the bench with a typewritten document in his hand.

'Ladies and gentlemen of the jury,' the judge said. 'In view of the testimony you have heard in this case and in view of the fact also that there is no evidence presented to contradict the testimony you heard, the Court will direct you to sign the following form of verdict.'

He then proceeded to read from the paper as the jury watched him, relaxed now, aware that the fate of the silent, young, black man was not to be in their hands at all.

'We, the jury,' Napoli read, 'find the petitioner, Donald Lang, was at the time of the empanelling of this jury, and is

47

now, physically incompetent to stand trial.'

He then handed the paper to the clerk and instructed the jury to sign it. The paper was passed from juror to juror, signed by each and returned to the clerk where it was once again read aloud for the record.

The hearing was over. There remained only the decision of the court as to what would happen next to Donald Lang. There were no precedents to go by. The only case of a person as handicapped as Donald Lang held for a capital crime occurred in South Carolina in 1860. The outcome of that case was obscure and was of no help at all to Judge Napoli. But Illinois law was firm on one point. Under the Code of Criminal Procedure, Chapter 38, Article 104, a person found to be physically incompetent to stand trial must remain under the jurisdiction of the court. The law did not specify where such a person was to be held, nor for how long. It simply stated that once the person was found to be competent to stand trial, the proceedings pending against him would be resumed.

The question in everyone's mind was: Could Donald Lang ever become competent? Could he learn to understand the nature of the charge against him? Could he learn to communicate with his counsel?

Judge Napoli had little data on which to base an answer. Dr. Haines had diagnosed Donald Lang's condition as mutism but his report had also touched upon other facets of Donald's medical history which seemed to cast doubts on the young man's capacity for learning. Dr. Haines had included in his report information received from the Cook County Mental Health Clinic dated 4 December 1958. When Donald Lang was thirteen years old, he had broken his hand and had been admitted to the orthopaedic ward of the Illinois Research Hospital. The report read in part ...

'He (Donald Lang) was admitted to Cook County Mental Health Clinic on 4 December 1958, from Illinois Research Hospital. A diagnosis of "Deaf-Mutism-Acute Psychotic Reaction" was made. A secondary diagnosis of "Mental Deficiency with Psychosis" was also on the diagnosis. He had been in Illinois Research since 12 November 1958, because of a fractured hand. He was too erratic and unpredictable to be allowed in an unsupervised environment. He will attack physically anyone that frustrates him and did so on the Orthopaedic Service at the hospital. He would not obey the nurses nor would he stay in bed and take his medicine. He would kick the nurses and doctors who tried to restrain him. The mother was quite defensive and also protective of the patient, stating that he was no trouble when he was at home.'

Donald Lang was released from the Mental Health Clinic seven days after the diagnosis that he was both 'mentally deficient and psychotic'. He went home with his mother, a cast on his broken hand.

In October 1963, Donald Lang was arrested for stealing a truck that had been parked at the South Water Market. The keys had been left in it and Donald drove it home. According to his brother, and to the workmen who knew him at the market, Donald had always yearned to drive. The 'theft' of the truck had most probably been nothing more than the giving in to an overpowering urge, but it brought him into his first contact with a system of law that was not equipped to deal with the extraordinary individual. Because of his inability to speak, he was turned over to the Psychiatric Institute of the Municipal Court, certified a 'Schizophrenic-Paranoid Type' and committed to Jacksonville State Hospital for observation.

Dr. Haines' report to the court continued ...

'A report from Jacksonville State Hospital reveals that Donald Lang arrived there 12 December 1963. As he had been deaf from childhood and is unable to read lips, read sign language, unable to write and had no way except pointing to indicate his wishes, no formal testing was possible. A diagnosis of "Deaf Mutism with possible mental deficiency with behavioural reaction" was made. On 3 March 1964, he was seen at the Illinois School for the Deaf for a Mental, Hearing and Speech Evaluation. He was somewhat hostile during the mental examination and no normal test could be administered. According to their records, they first saw him in 1947. Educational history indicated that he had an I.Q. in the lower 50 or upper 60 range. When he was seen in March 1964, they were not able to provide the intensive and specialized training he needed at the School for the Deaf. During his entire hospitalization he showed no evidence of psychotic behaviour and was given an absolute discharge as without psychosis on 26 April 1964, and left the hospital accompanied by his mother.'

The evaluation of Donald Lang's mental capacity was inconsistent at best. Either he was mentally deficient or he was not. It was vital for the court to have an accurate, up-to-the-minute estimation of Donald Lang's potential ability to achieve competency in the eyes of the law. A trial that could only have been a travesty of justice had been avoided by ruling Donald Lang physically incompetent to stand trial, but that decision had placed him in limbo. It had bound him to the court, or, more specifically, to the Cook County Jail. This was primarily a holding facility where men accused of crimes waited for their day in court and a verdict that would either set them free or send them on to a State penitentiary. Donald Lang was languishing in that jail now, waiting for a trial that might never take place. His brief appearance in court had done nothing but push him deeper into a legal *cul-de-sac*.

A chain of events now began that would have a profound effect on the life of Donald Lang and Lowell Myers. It began on the morning of 21 February 1966, in Judge Napoli's court. Assistant State's Attorney Charles Barish filed a motion.

'Your petitioner prays this Honourable Court to appoint Dr. Helmer R. Myklebust, Director of the Institute of Language Disorders of the North-western University, Evanston, Illinois, to examine the defendant on Wednesday, 23 February 1966 at said Institute. Your petitioner further prays that after said examination by Dr. Myklebust that he file a report in this Court by 16 March 1966.'

'If the Court so signs this order,' Barish said, 'I have arranged for Mr. Lang to be examined on Wednesday of this week, on the 23rd, at nine o'clock in the morning. The order calls for the sheriff to deliver Mr. Lang to Doctor Myklebust at the North-western University campus in Evanston, where the examination will take approximately most of the day, five or six hours, then to be returned.'

Lowell Myers protested. 'Your Honour, I object to this motion on the grounds that this is a matter which has already been passed upon by the jury. This is an attempt to make a collateral attack upon the jury's verdict. However, if you do grant this motion, I would like the order modified to provide that I can be present at the examination, because I think I should be present at every proceeding which affects the defendant.'

'Your Honour,' Barish said, 'I have taken the initiative to ask Doctor Myklebust as to the possibility of having outsiders or observers present, and Doctor Myklebust tells me, in view of the fact that the defendant is in custody, the sheriff and perhaps Mr. Myers, if he so wishes, could be present at the examination, but only by virtue of looking through a one-way glass into the room where Doctor Myklebust will conduct the examination.

'I don't know exactly what procedure the doctor will take in the examination, but I don't believe he will be able to conduct it if Mr. Myers is present in the same room, but I believe he will be able to look into the room and, perhaps, even hear. I am not certain of that.'

The irony of the statement was not lost on Myers, but he made no comment. His proficiency at lip reading led many people to forget his handicap.

Barish, a genial, compassionate man, had been on the case from the beginning, from the day that Judge Napoli had called him into chambers and said, *Charley, what the hell do we do? Don't look for precedents, I don't think there are any.'*

It had been Barish who had first contacted Lowell Myers when Napoli had been reluctant to hand the case to the Public Defender's office. Now Barish was trying to explain his reasoning for turning Donald over to Dr. Myklebust—a move that did not meet with Myers' approval in any way.

'We are merely trying to assist the Court in the determination of any further proceedings as to trial, commitment, or whatever it might be. This is not a collateral attack, merely an aid to the Court on behalf of the people.'

Myers looked dubious, but he had nothing further to say. Judge Napoli then rendered his decision.

'I'm going to sign this order,' Napoli said, 'because it is essential that we get a further examination in this case. The question of whether or not he could communicate is going to be the crux of the situation, to eventually determine whether or not he could be placed on trial for the crime of murder on which he is indicted, or whether this Court may have to take some other steps to make any disposition of the case. I don't see where your client's rights are going to be prejudiced in any

way, Mr. Myers. Order for the examination by Doctor Myklebust is entered as per draft order.'

Further hearing in the case was then deferred to 16 March
1966, at ten o'clock in the morning.

On 23 February Donald Lang was removed from Cook County
Jail and driven north to Evanston and the sprawling campus of
North-western University. There, without Lowell Myers being
present, he was examined by Dr. Myklebust. Using pure tone
audiometry tests, Dr. Myklebust determined the extent of
Donald's deafness and classified him as having profound sensori-neural deafness with no usable residual hearing in either
ear. Any doubts that Donald Lang had been faking the extent
of his handicap could now be set at rest. He was deaf as a
stone. Dr Myklebust was also positive in his findings regarding
Donald's intellectual capacities, and it was this evaluation that
would have such far-reaching consequences.

These excerpts are from Dr. Myklebust's letter to Judge
Napoli, dated 1 March 1966.

'... As determined by several nonverbal measures of intelligence, we have no question but that Donald's mental capacity does not exceed that of seven or eight years. In some
respects, because of his super-imposed handicap of profound
deafness, his ability to function intellectually falls between
six and seven years. This means that he is mentally deficient
and cannot under any circumstances be considered capable
of independent, self-sufficient, responsible behaviour in
society. I stress that this mental deficiency is not caused
by his deafness, but rather that he is a multiple-handicapped
person, being both deaf and mentally deficient.'

The prognosis was depressing in its finality.

'... Persons deaf from early life who also evidence the degree
of mental deficiency found in Donald characteristically are
not able to acquire language. This means that Donald's inability to communicate is a further manifestation of his
severe deafness and his marked mental retardation.

In addition to being mentally deficient and profoundly
deaf, Donald presents a problem of hostility and aggressiveness which further complicates his circumstances. This means
that his inferior emotional adjustment also must be considered when disposition is determined.

Because of our long experience in examining and working with individuals with limited verbal facility, we did not
find it difficult to obtain diagnostic results as stated above and
we have no question of their validity. Therefore, it is clear
that Donald is intellectually incompetent and cannot be
held accountable for his actions. Rather, it is urgent that
disposition include appropriate institutionalization. There is
no other practical means whereby he can be prevented from
being a victim or from further victimizing others.'

Further victimizing? There was no record of Donald Lang
ever having victimized anyone. He stood accused of Ernestine
Williams' murder, but in the eyes of the law, he was innocent
until proven otherwise. It was Lowell Myers' belief that Donald
had not killed Ernestine, that he had simply been there—an
innocent bystander and a convenient scapegoat. As for Donald's
intellectual capacity, was it possible for a person with a six-
year-old mentality to function the way Donald had functioned
for years at the South Water Market? To drive and repair a
forklift jeep? To learn to drive a truck simply by watching how
the truck drivers manipulated gear shift and clutch? Perhaps
it was possible, but Lowell Myers felt otherwise. As for Donald's
'hostility and aggressiveness', this only seemed to manifest
itself when Donald was placed in circumstances that were
alien to him. He had kicked out at the nurses at Illinois Research Hospital and had shown aggressive tendencies during
the five-hour ordeal of being tested by Dr. Myklebust; but at
home, or at work on the loading docks, he had been noted as
a mild, even-tempered, happy individual. Had Donald Lang
been by nature a hostile and aggressive person, there had certainly been ample opportunity to demonstrate it. The ABLA
Housing Project had a high rate of juvenile crime, and yet in
all the years that Donald had lived there, he had never been
counted among its delinquents. While other boys his age had
fought rock and bottle fights in the nearby alleys, Donald had
waited outside markets to help old women home with their
packages. He had been almost a storybook youngster, sharing
cookies and candies with children in the streets, always eager
to run an errand or fix a broken bicycle. A nice, young boy
who had become a nice, young man. No trouble to the police.
No trouble to anyone. An almost impossible statement for any
youth in the black ghetto of Chicago.

But there was no reason to doubt the validity of the report from Dr. Myklebust. The examination had been thorough, conducted by a renowned expert under optimum conditions using the latest scientific equipment. Assistant State's Attorney Barish was prepared to move for a new competency hearing.

Lowell Myers was also prepared for the 16 March hearing before Judge Napoli. There was no jury present, only Myers, Charles Barish—and Donald Lang.

'Your Honour,' Myers said, 'I have some motions which I am going to present to the Court at this time. My first motion is a motion to dismiss the indictment because four months have gone by and Donald Lang has been in jail for more than four months. He has not been tried, and so I have a motion here that the indictment shall be dismissed under the terms of the statute.'

Barish cut in quickly. 'Your Honour, I would like to be heard on this matter briefly.'

'Who's making the motion?' Judge Napoli snapped. 'Are you making the motion or is he making it?'

The State's Attorney stood abashed. 'I thought he was through.'

'If he is making the motion, he has got the right to talk first.'

Judge Napoli seemed impatient, almost testy. The matter of the State versus Donald Lang was not a case that any judge in Cook County would have handled out of choice. It was a case that the young lawyers in the State's Attorney's office were calling a 'lulu!' and it was highly probable that the transcripts pertaining to State versus Lang would be read and reread for many reasons. No infractions of the rules of court procedure would, or could, be tolerated.

'What is the basis of your motion, Mr. Myers?' Napoli asked.

'This is my basis, your Honour. Donald Lang was arrested on 12 November 1965, and more than one hundred and twenty days have elapsed and he has been in custody continuously for that time and he has not been brought to trial. So, under the terms of the statute, we move to dismiss the indictment.'

'Have you read the statute?'

'I have, your Honour.'

'Well, I would like to hear it. I would like to hear the code. Let's read it again.'

Section 103, sub-section 5, of the Illinois Criminal Law and Procedural Code, sub-section (a) was then read by Lowell Myers.

It stated that any person in custody for an alleged offence had to be tried within one hundred and twenty days from the date he had been taken into custody unless the delay was occasioned by the defendant, by a competency hearing, or by an interlocutory appeal.

Judge Napoli pondered the words for a moment. 'Well, what about the provision ... "Unless delay is occasioned by a competency hearing"? That takes it out of the four-month period, Mr. Myers.'

'That is correct, your Honour, if the delay is occasioned by the defendant, but the competency hearing only took one day.'

'I know how long it took!' Napoli shot back. 'The record shows how long it took, but we have not concluded at this time as to a disposition of that matter.'

'Your Honour,' Myers said, 'we are seeking the Court to enter its judgment based upon the verdict which was rendered.'

'That's right,' said Napoli. 'Do you want to say something on this matter, Mr. Barish?'

The opening gambits were over.

'Your Honour,' Barish said, 'the motion we are presenting today is a motion for a new competency hearing wherein I ask that because of the report submitted by Doctor Myklebust pursuant to order of the Court, that there has been newly-discovered evidence pertaining to the question of Donald Lang's *mental capacity* and because of this newly-acquired evidence we are going to ask for a new competency hearing.'

Myers sought to block this motion by offering the Court a motion of his own. A jury had found Donald Lang to be *physically incompetent to stand trial*, and he wished the Court to abide by that jury's verdict. A legal memorandum was attached to his motion that the Court render judgment. The two-page, typewritten document was handed to Judge Napoli. It read:

The Facts of this Case
Donald Lang is a deaf-mute. A jury had held that he is physically unable to stand trial, due to his handicaps. His physical handicaps are permanent. Therefore, the trial will never be held.

Donald Lang cannot be ordered to spend his life in jail.

Donald Lang will be 'waiting' for his trial for the rest of his lifetime (about 50 years). The question that this Court must now decide is: *Where* does he do his waiting? Can the

55

State put him in jail for 50 years to wait for a trial that will never take place? The answer is NO! Obviously, a man cannot be put in jail for life merely on suspicion. There is no law in this State permitting such a thing to be done—and such things have not been done in civilized countries SINCE THE MIDDLE AGES ... The inevitable conclusion is that the man must be set free, and he will 'wait' for his trial as he goes about his daily work and his usual occupations. *Likewise, Donald Lang cannot be ordered into a mental institution to wait for a trial.*

Just as Donald Lang cannot be compelled to wait in jail for ever for a trial that will never take place, likewise, he cannot be ordered to spend his life in a mental institution waiting for such a trial. He cannot be put into a mental institution merely because he has a *physical* handicap.

A mental institution cannot be used as a substitute for a jail to 'put away' someone whose presence is considered inconvenient or troublesome to the State.

It should be noted that there is not one *single word* in the entire record of this case which says that Donald Lang is *mentally ill* in any manner. In view of this record, I submit that it would be grossly incorrect to order this man committed to a mental institution.

The Necessary Result

Donald Lang has not been found guilty of anything. No one has any legal right to imprison him in any manner. It must be kept in mind that our entire legal system was carefully devised to preserve liberty, *at whatever cost.* Our system is based on the premise that: 'it is better for ten guilty men to go free, rather than one innocent man should be imprisoned.

The *inevitable* result of our legal system is that Donald Lang must be set free. No one has any power or right to imprison him—in *any* manner.

The Court must order his release ...

Lowell Myers handed a copy of this document to Judge Napoli.

'I would like one copy of that motion to be filed in the record of the case, Your Honour, to show what the defendant's position is.'

Judge Napoli passed the copy to the clerk of the Court.

'It may be filed, Mr. Myers.'

'Now,' Myers went on, 'I have prepared a draft order which I am going to offer to the Court and it says that judgment is entered upon the jury's verdict and that the defendant is discharged from the custody of the sheriff because, Your Honour, if he cannot be tried, if we have a jury's verdict that he cannot be tried, what disposition does the Court make of him? Either he is kept in custody for life or he is released. A decision must be made.'

Myers had clarified the dilemma of the Court. It was new ground for everyone. There was nothing in the long and honourable profession of law that could be used as a guideline at that point. Judge Napoli knew it—and so did Myers. The freeing of Donald Lang because he was *physically* incapable of standing trial would establish a precedent that could be open to infinite interpretations. Judge Napoli was reluctant to step off into the great unknown.

'Judgment will be held in abeyance at this time for the reason that the State is filing a motion. Mr. Barish has already indicated that they are asking for another competency hearing in view of a report submitted by Doctor Myklebust of Northwestern University. So I will withhold entering judgment at this point. The motion of the State for a competency hearing is the next thing.'

'No, Your Honour,' Myers said. 'I would like to make one more motion.'

'Very well, Mr. Myers. I will hear your motion first. Then we will pass on the State's motion.'

'This is the motion, Your Honour, on behalf of the defendant demanding to be placed on trial for murder.'

If Judge Napoli had not been looking at Donald Lang before, he did so now. The young man's expression had not changed. He was totally unaware of the astounding proposal his attorney was making.

'Your Honour,' Myers continued, 'we believe on behalf of the defendant that he is not guilty and that he wants to go home. If the only way he can go home is to be placed on trial for murder, then he wishes to be placed on trial for murder, and on behalf of the defendant, I offer to waive the protection of the Illinois statutes on his behalf. I offer to waive the jury verdict in his behalf. I ask the Court to place him on trial immediately.'

57

The judge was understandably flabbergasted. It was a desperate stratagem. As no trial date had been set on the murder indictment, Myers had not been permitted to examine the police evidence against his client. He did not know what they had against Donald Lang.

'By what authority do you assume that you have the right to waive all these things, including the verdict of the jury?' Judge Napoli wanted to know.

'Your Honour,' Myers said, 'as his attorney I am required to take those steps which are in his best interests and it is I who determine what those steps are. No one else, your Honour.'

'Is it your contention that any lawyer or even the *Court* could waive the question of competency?'

'That is for the Court to decide. I present the motion. Let the Court decide on it.'

The Motion to waive Donald Lang's rights was denied. A mental competency hearing would take place.

31 March 1966. Again Donald Lang sat silently in Judge Napoli's court, facing a panel of twelve jurors. He had been in the Cook County Jail for nearly five months. They had been months of waiting without knowing what he was waiting for. Months of confinement in a crowded cell block, surrounded by the muggers and the rapists and the killers of the city. There had been no special treatment for Donald Lang; he had been just another prisoner. A fellow inmate on the tier remembered him as a loner who spent most of his time leaning against a wall with his arms folded, watching the activity in the dayroom but taking no part in it. He ate well and would take a shower if the shower was pointed out to him. He had survived by aping the behaviour of others. But as a person he had remained an enigma.

Dr. William H. Haines described his first meeting with Donald in jail ...

'He is a thin, short, untidy, defective male. When questioned he will make guttural sounds in a high eunuch type of a voice. To most questions, he will nod his head. He nodded his head to questions such as, "Can you talk the sign language—where do you live—are you a girl—what is your name." He was given a piece of paper to write his name and he took the pencil and held the paper against the wall.'

The copy of Donald's 'handwriting' was submitted to the Court. It was simply a jumble of meaningless scrawls. Dr. Haines had given testimony as to Donald's physical incompetence at the 20 January hearing, now he testified at the new hearing.

'I examined the defendant Donald Lang in December 1965,' Dr. Haines said under direct examination by Charles Barish. 'I was unable to communicate with him because of his physical condition. I re-examined the defendant in January of 1966, in the Cook County Jail. I found that he was unable to co-operate with his counsel and he did not know the nature of the charge against him. In my opinion, he is a mental defective. He is a mute. Even if he could speak, it would be my opinion that he would be a mental defective.'

Q. Doctor Haines, do you know, of your own knowledge, as to the intelligence quotient of Donald Lang?

A. No, I don't. From information I have received, Donald Lang's I.Q. is low. I have examined other deaf-mutes and I have diagnosed them to be mentally competent. My present opinion of the defendant is that he is incompetent at this time. It is mental incompetency.

Lowell Myers rose to cross-examine him. Dr. Haines' testimony had not changed much since the first hearing—except for his opinion on Donald's mental capacity. The words ... 'it is mental incompetency' hung in the courtroom like a dark cloud.

Did Dr. Haines recall being asked what his diagnosis was of Donald's condition on the 20th of January?

'I presume so,' Dr. Haines said.

Q. And did you reply in one word and say 'mutism'?

A. I could have. My present opinions relative to Donald Lang are not inconsistent with any previous opinions I have had. On that day, I was not asked any direct questions relative to the *mental* capacity of Donald Lang. My previous opinion of Donald Lang's competency was not inconsistent with my present opinion of his mental capacity. It is my opinion today, as before, that he does not know the nature of the charge against him and cannot co-operate with his counsel. I diagnose him as a mental defective.

Dr. Haines was excused and Helmer R. Myklebust was called to the stand by the State's Attorney. This was the State's key witness and Barish placed great stress on impressing the jury with Dr. Myklebust's qualifications. They were considerable.

Q. Doctor Myklebust, what position do you occupy on the staff of North-western University?

A. I'm a professor of language pathology in the School of Speech, a professor of psychology in the College of Arts and Sciences, a professor of neurology and psychiatry in the Medical School. I am the director of the Institute of Language Disorders and have directed it since its beginnings nearly fifteen years ago.

Q. Do you belong to any professional organizations?

A. Yes. I am a member of the Illinois Psychological Association, the Midwestern Psychological Association, the American Psychological Association. I am a member of several organizations for handicapped children, I am an honourable member of the Conference of the Executives of the American Schools for the Deaf and an associate member of the American Academy of Neurology—among others.

Dr. Myklebust was also the author of several books on the deaf, from diagnosis to treatment. In the course of his long career he had examined and diagnosed thousands of persons for speech impairment and mental capacity. He was an impressive witness with unimpeachable credentials.

Q. Doctor, on what occasion did you first have to meet Donald Lang?

A. He was referred to the centre which I direct by a vocational rehabilitation agency in January 1962. An examination was made at that time.

Q. Doctor, would you tell the ladies and gentlemen of the jury what form this examination took?

A. The examination was conducted by members of my staff, and it included mental ability, social maturity, ability to communicate, aptitude hearing and motor ability.

Q. Doctor, did you formulate an opinion as to the mental capacity of Donald Lang at that time?

A. Yes, we did. Our diagnosis was that he was seriously mentally retarded and that he should not be expected to make an adjustment in society, like the average, normal deaf person could make, but that he should have supervision.

Q. Doctor, did you at that time make any suggestions, relative to the future of Donald Lang?

A. Yes. We said that he should not be expected to be successful, in the usual manner, because of his mental retardation, and that he should be supervised.

Q. Now, you say you made a study of Donald Lang recently. Doctor, would you tell the ladies and gentlemen of the jury and the Court what took place at the Institute on 23 February 1966—what the examination consisted of and what was done, if anything.

A. Yes. This examination was done by me personally.

Lowell Myers raised an objection, an objection that he did not feel could be voiced in front of the jury. He waited patiently while the jury members filed out of the box for a short recess. When they had left the courtroom, Myers said:

'Your Honour, I'm going to object to having the doctor testify as to what happened on 23 February 1966, on the grounds that Donald Lang's attorney was not permitted to be present at the examination.'

The objection had been expected by Judge Napoli. Dr. Myklebust had stipulated that no one but himself be permitted in the examining room while he was testing Donald Lang. Myers could come to the University, but only to view the proceedings through a glass panel. That had not been acceptable to Myers. He had objected in February just as he objected now. Both objections were overruled—the examination of Donald had been allowed to take place without Myers being present, and Dr. Myklebust's testimony was permitted to be heard. The jury was brought back and Barish resumed his questioning of the witness.

Q. What did the examination of Donald Lang consist of, Doctor?

A. I administered tests of a kind used for persons who do not have language. The tests consist of problems and tasks, like assembling or drawing, or imitating. I tested motor co-ordination, hearing, social maturity, and manual dexterity and strength. My opinion on the basis of my examination is that the defendant's mental capacity falls at about seven years. He is a higher level imbecile. He does not have the mental capacity to understand the indictment against him or to co-operate with his counsel. It is my opinion that his mental deficiency is separate from his deafness and he is mentally incompetent.

Donald Lang sat slouched in his chair—bored, restless. The totally deaf are often bored and restless when events are going on around them that they can neither hear nor comprehend. The jury looked at Donald Lang who had just been referred to as an imbecile. There was nothing in the young man's attitude or appearance to make them doubt the definition.

The State had finished their questioning of Dr. Myklebust and Myers rose to cross-examine.

Q. Doctor Myklebust, did you make records of what you did?

A. Yes.

Q. Do you have with you the records that you prepared during the examination?

A. Yes, I do.

Q. How old is Donald?

A. He is twenty years.

Q. What was the first test that you gave him?

A. The first tests were some drawing tests. He was to draw human figures and a certain geometric design.

Q. What was the next test that you gave him after the drawing test?

A. Well, I cannot give you a sequence of test by test for that afternoon. I don't think I could do it, even if I referred to the records. We keep all of the test records, but we don't necessarily follow the same sequence and I could not give you the whole sequence at this time.

Q. How many tests did you give him?

A. Seventeen. Some of the mental tests are the type where he is shown a design and he builds the design before him with blocks. There are tests where he looks at pictures and must decide whether two pictures are alike or not alike. Another type of test is commonly called a maze. There are a whole series of these, but each is on a separate sheet of paper, and he is to find the route through the maze by using a pencil to indicate the route he chooses.

Q. Is it true that the identification of mentally deficient people, through the use of psychological tests, presents a very complex problem?

A. Yes. It's a complex problem.

Q. And isn't it true that there are many sources of error in the use of tests?

A. No. I can't agree with your statement.

Q. I'm going to prove it to you from a book written by a Doctor Helmer Myklebust called *Auditory Disorders*. Did you write that book?

A. Yes.

Q. Well, on Page 241 of that book, and I quote, 'there are many sources of errors in tests.' Did you write that?

Dr. Myklebust seemed taken aback. His reply to the question was garbled and unclear.

A. Yes, Counsel. If I must answer directly, I must say 'no.' I think, if you will read it back, that's what my reply was. If you will permit me to elaborate, then I will give you some reasons for the statement. It's a little different statement.

Myers felt that he had made his point. He had shown a degree of inconsistency in the doctor's testimony, but he did not belabour it. He went directly to other matters.

Q. After you gave him the tests, did you speak to the jailers here in the jail to find out how he had actually been acting in the jail?

A. No.

Q. Did you speak to any of his relatives to find out what his behaviour has been recently with his relatives?

A. No.

Q. Did you go to the place where he was previously working and ask the people he was working with what his behaviour had been?

Barish raised an objection before Dr. Myklebust could say one more 'No'. Myers had no more questions to ask and the State rested its case.

Myers then took the stand as the first witness for Donald Lang. He had made it clear to the jury before the start of the hearing that he was not going to call experts to testify on Donald's behalf. He intended to produce people who had known Donald for many years, people who could tell the Court about Donald Lang the *person*, not Donald Lang the bewildered 'imbecile' struggling through a maze test. Speaking slowly and deliberately, Myers told the jury of his first meeting with his client on 5th January of that year.

'I examined Donald Lang in order to find out whether I could communicate with him. I found that he is a deaf-mute, he has never been educated, he cannot read nor write, he does not know sign language, he has never been taught to lip read.

There is only one way to communicate with him. That is by the use of what are called basic signs—pointing, drawing pictures, acting it out.

'By using basic signs, I was able to communicate with him a little bit. The first thing I wanted to communicate with him was whether or not he wanted to go home. In order to do that, I had to go to his home first and see what it looked like. And then I came back and I drew a picture of it, and I pointed to the home and I made the sign, in the deaf-mute language, for the word *home*, and I repeated that for a while and I believe that he got the idea. I pointed to him and I made the sign *home* and he nodded *yes*. He communicated that he wanted to go home. That took about twenty minutes. And then I tried to see if I could communicate to him—*do you want a cup of coffee?* And, to do that, I had to teach him the word for coffee, and I had to draw a picture of a cup of coffee, and I believe he understood me and he indicated *no*. And that took twenty minutes.

'I then asked him if he wanted to see his sister. And, by the same process of sign and drawing I was able to communicate the sign for sister and he indicated *yes*, he wanted to see his sister. And that took about twenty minutes.

'Now, that is communication. That is learning. I only taught him three or four words in an hour, but it's my belief that if you kept it up, an hour or two a day, the words would accumulate. When you got to five hundred words, you would talk to him. It is my opinion, based upon my observation of him and my experience in the field, that he can be educated. It would take time, but there are special schools where they educate deaf-mute people, where they can do it ten times better than I can do it.

'I gave him another test. I took my pen and I took it to pieces. I said—*you put it back together* and I indicated all the parts and he put it back together very quickly, much quicker than I could have. It is my opinion that his mind is good. He has a quick mind.'

'Objection, Your Honour,' Barish called out. 'There is no foundation for that opinion. Counsel is not a doctor.'

'Let it stand,' Judge Napoli said.

Lowell Myers continued: 'On 17 February, I saw Donald again and I drew a picture of the School of Speech at Northwestern, where I have been many times, and I attempted to communicate to him that I did not want him to co-operate with Doctor Myklebust, that he should not do it, that he should refuse, and I believe that he understood me.'

Myers was attempting to plant in the jury's mind that Donald had done badly on the tests because of this prior instruction to be non-co-operative. There was no indication that the jury believed this and Barish, in his cross-examination of Myers, chose to ignore the statement. His cross-examination was short and to the point:

Q. Mr. Myers, have you had any special training relative to the study of nervous and mental disorders?

A. I have had none.

Q. Mr. Myers, have you had occasion previously to attempt to make a diagnosis of the mental capacity of any person?

A. Yes. I do that quite frequently.

Q. Yet you have no special talent for this. Mr. Myers, the opinion you stated, is that based upon any degree of training or medical certainty?

A. I have never been trained in psychology in school, but I have read the subject.

The words—*I have read the subject*—would be weighed by the jury against Dr. Myklebust's long list of titles and degrees.

William Lang, Jr., took the stand and Myers asked his questions about his brother that were designed to show that, outside of his being a deaf-mute, Donald was a normal human being.

Q. Have you worked with him?

A. Yes. He's helped me work on my car, he's helped me do various carpentry things in the home, plus he's self-sufficient on his own. He works and supports his own self.

Q. What did he do with the money he made from working?

A. He bought his own clothes and he used some for various recreational pleasures. He likes movies and he's also a member of the YMCA at Monroe and Ashland. He likes basketball, volleyball and swimming.

Q. What is Donald's handicap? What is his difficulty?

A. He's a deaf-mute. He can't hear and he can't talk.

Q. Did he ever go to school?

A. He went to school for one month, when he was five-and-a-half years old. The reason we had to take him out of school is because he was having trouble with personal hygiene, as far as going to the washroom. This was the reason he was out of school.

Q. In your more than twenty years of living with him, what is your opinion as to his mentality?

A. My opinion is that Donald's mental capacity is very good. He's quick. You show him what you want done and he'll do it. He's lacking in education, he's never been to school, and this automatically brings on a problem because he's lacking in education.

Q. How does he learn things?

A. Well, any time you want Donald to learn something, you show it to him once and explain it to him and from then on you have no trouble, he'll do it whenever you want it.

Q. What's his temperament like ... his personality?

A. His personality is very good. We have no trouble with him, and our neighbours have never had any trouble with him.

Q. Would you like to have him come back and live with you?

A. Yes.

Two more witnesses followed—Mary Lang, Donald's stepmother, and Arnell Nelson, a friend of the family. Their testimony followed the same line as William's—Donald as a handicapped, but functioning, individual.

'He wants to live the normal life,' Mary Lang said. 'But he doesn't know how to put into oral phrases as to what he wants, but people around him understand his wants and desires. I think that Donald has equipment to work with, but he hasn't had the professional educational guidance that he should have had to put his actions into effort.'

'Donald buys his own clothes,' Arnell Nelson said. 'He participates in sports, he likes to go to ball games and movies. I would say that he is normal in every respect except that he is a deaf-mute.'

There was no doubting the honesty of these witnesses. Their sincerity was evident and the State's cross-examination of them was low-keyed and gentle. And then it was all over. There were no more witnesses to be heard. The defence rested its case and the State had no rebuttal. The attorneys would now present their final arguments to the jury.

'Place the evidence on a scale,' Barish advised the jurors.

'Weigh the scales, weigh the testimony, think of the quality of the testimony that was presented.'

Barish had been a prosecutor for a long time. He was at ease and comfortable in front of a jury and knew what points to stress so that they could weigh one thing against another. He hammered away at the difference between the 'expert' testimony of doctors Myklebust and Haines and the 'layman' testimony of Myers and his three witnesses.

'The State presented eminent medical testimony, the only type of testimony that one can give great weight to. We cannot take the opinion of a layman. We must accept it for what it is worth. The State presented two *experts*, qualified individuals, specializing in the field of nervous and mental disorders.'

And the testimony that Donald functioned? That he worked ... bought his own clothes ... went to ball games and played basketball at the YMCA?

'Mr. William Lang said that his brother is active in sports. I have no quarrel with that. It's probably true that he's physically sound, as far as his body, that he is a strong individual. He works. He takes boxes from the ground and puts them on a truck, and from the truck he puts them on the ground. He loads and unloads. He does physical, menial tasks. Can he do more? What are the mental abilities of a child of six, seven or eight? If they had money, they could buy candy and ice cream and perhaps clothing. He says that Donald can fix a car, Donald can do carpentry work. I have an eight-year-old son and he helps me with the car. He doesn't help me fix the carburettor, but he helps me clean it, he helps me wash it. If I want to clean the air filter, I say, "David, unscrew the top." I ask my son to help me with some carpentry—"Drive the nail in here ... hold a piece of wood for me." He can do it, Donald can do it. What more than these basic, menial skills can Donald do? Does he have the mental capacity to go beyond that? They said that he could go out on the streets and mingle. Well, so can children mingle. Weigh the scales, weigh the testimony, think of the *quality* of the testimony that was presented. And, on the basis of the evidence that was presented by the State, I feel that you will return a verdict finding Donald Lang is mentally incompetent to stand trial.'

Lowell Myers knew that he could not tear down the State's arguments nor demolish the testimony that had been presented. Dr. Myklebust and Dr. Haines were not quacks, their reputations were *bona fide*, their degrees were real. All that Myers could do was to chip away at their testimony—not to discredit it, but to cast doubts on its omniscience.

'Ladies and gentlemen of the jury ... the prosecutor talked about the opinions of his two experts. Now, every case has a key, and the key to this case is to understand the difference between facts and opinions.

'Suppose you ask me—*do you know how old that man is?* That's a factual question, is it not? I give you a factual answer —*I don't know.* But suppose you say—*what is your opinion?* What's my opinion? I can answer anything in the world! *My opinion is that he is ninety-five ... my opinion is that he's twenty-one ...* I don't say it's right. It's my opinion, that's all.

'Doctor Haines testified to two significant facts. I asked him a factual question—*Do you know what Donald's mental quotient is? His I.Q.?* That's a factual question and he gave me a factual answer—*No.* Doctor Haines is in a position to tell you what Donald's behaviour has been since November, while he's been in jail. I asked him—*Do you agree that he's not aggressive and that he gets along well?* He agrees with that. That is something that he knows about—He's not aggressive and he gets along well.

'Were there any other factual statements that were significant? I ask him about Donald's mentality—he does not know. I ask him about Donald in jail—he's getting along fine. The rest is opinion. I asked him—*What was your diagnosis on 20 January?* And he said—*Mutism.* That's all, mutism, nothing about Donald's mentality. Has he examined Donald after 20 January? No, he never examined him again. Well, he has a right to change his opinion. Anybody can. Today one way and tomorrow another way. That's up to him. I can't stop him.

'Let's talk about Doctor Myklebust. Now, what are the basic facts that Doctor Myklebust knows, leaving the opinions out of it for the time being? I asked him—*How old is Donald?* He said—*Twenty.* That is a factual question and that is a factual answer. He said he was with Donald for three hours. That's a basic fact. He was with Donald for three hours. Now, let's get to those opinions. He gave Donald tests. I told Donald not to take those tests. There was no reason for them. If a man doesn't co-operate can you give him a valid test? Obviously, you can't. I said to him—*Isn't it true that there were many sources for error in using those tests?* He said—*No.* Well, he's contradicting himself. In his own book, he wrote that there were many sources for error in the use of tests!

'There is only one fact that Doctor Myklebust testified to that we can check up on, to see how accurate he is. I said— *How old is Donald?* He said—*Twenty*. He's wrong. Donald is twenty-one! I knew he would be wrong. You can ask him things, concrete things that you can check on, and he will be wrong about it. That's how careful and accurate he is. I said—*What's the second test you gave to Donald?* He couldn't even tell us what the second test he gave to Donald was, if there was a second test.

'Do you remember Doctor Myklebust, when they put him on the witness stand, when he was going on giving us his opinion, and I started asking him about the facts? What is the first test and the second test and what is it composed of? And the more I asked him about the facts, the more uncomfortable he became. Isn't that true? He looked very peculiar when I was asking him about the facts. I asked him about the first test and the second test and he doesn't like that at all. Doctor Myklebust was with Donald for three hours. We have three people here who were with Donald for years and years. You talk about experts at work, experts about Donald? The people around him are experts on Donald. Myklebust is an expert on opinions.'

A trial lawyer talks and the jury listens. There is no way of knowing what the jury is thinking. Counsel may reach heights of oratorical magnificence, but a jury rarely gives outward signs that they have been moved by it. They sit and listen, their faces impassive. Have they already made up their minds? Counsel never knows, he can only talk, and hope that his words will have some effect on the outcome. Lowell Myers made his final plea for a verdict of mental competency for Donald Lang, and then Charles Barish, because he represented the petitioner in the case, had the privilege of making the closing argument.

'Now ladies and gentlemen, Mr. Myers says—*what are opinions? Opinions are of no value ... what are the facts?* Do any of us know all the facts of every situation that we are confronted with in our everyday life or do we base our experiences in life on our opinions—what we know, what people tell us, what we read, what we learn? We then formulate, we rationalize, we use our mind. We are trying to present to you, ladies and gentlemen of the jury, situations, testimony, circumstances for you to formulate an opinion. Mr. Myers said we don't want opinions, yet he is asking for yours and so is the petitioner. We are asking for your opinion.'

The State rested. It was now up to the twelve men and women in the jury box.

'Ladies and gentlemen,' Judge Napoli said, 'the Court will now instruct you as to the law in this case.

'I instruct you, the jury, that the law presumes every man to be sane, until the contrary is shown.

'You are the sole judges of the credibility of the witnesses and of the weight to be given to the testimony of each of them.

'In considering the evidence in this case, you are not required to set aside your own observation and experience in the affairs of life.

'In determining any of the questions of fact presented in this case, you should be governed solely by the evidence introduced before you.

'The Court instructs the jury as a matter of law that you shall find the defendant, Donald Lang, is mentally incompetent to stand trial if you believe from the evidence that the defendant, Donald Lang, because of a mental condition is unable to understand the nature and purpose of the proceedings against him or unable to assist in his defence.

'The jury may now retire to deliberate upon their verdict.'

Albert H. Chapman, official court reporter of the Circuit Court of Cook County, County Department—Criminal Division— waited along with everybody else for the jury's return. When they had reached a verdict, the bailiffs led them from the jury room and into the court. Albert H. Chapman then recorded the following:

THE COURT: Ladies and gentlemen, have you reached a verdict?

THE FOREMAN: Yes, we have, your Honour.

THE COURT: Will you hand it to the bailiff? And the bailiff will give it to the clerk.

THE CLERK: 'We, the jury, find the defendant, Donald Lang, was mentally incompetent at the time of the empanelling of the jury and now is mentally incompetent.'

THE COURT: Record the verdict, Mr. Clerk.

Judge Napoli moved swiftly, ruling on the verdict five days later. Combining the results of both hearings, he said ...

'It is therefore ordered and adjudged that the said Donald Lang is now physically and mentally incompetent and judgment on these verdicts is now entered.

'It is further ordered and adjudged that the Sheriff of Cook County take the defendant from the bar of this court to the common jail of Cook County, thence to the Illinois Security Hospital at Chester, Illinois, and there to deliver the said Donald Lang to the Department of Mental Health of the State of Illinois at said institution.

'It is further ordered and adjudged that the said Donald Lang be confined in said institution, as provided by the law of the State of Illinois, until he shall have fully and permanently recovered from his mental incompetency.'

Donald Lang, deaf-mute, was sentenced to a hospital for the criminally insane for what could well be the rest of his natural life.

Indictment Number 65–3421 had been satisfactorily resolved.

CHAPTER V

Lawyers and doctors tend to be philosophic in defeat. A client is found guilty—a patient dies on the operating table. What sustains professional men under such circumstances is the conviction that they had done their best. The evidence was overwhelming—the cancer too far advanced. On to the next case.

Lowell Myers had done his best for Donald Lang. He had done far more than any overworked public defender would have done for the standard two hundred and fifty dollar fee. He could give up on Donald Lang with a clear conscience and move on to other cases; but Lowell Myers decided to fight. The thought of Donald being sent to Chester dismayed him. The place was, purely and simply, an insane asylum, a maximum security institution, far stricter than any jail. What help could Donald receive in such a place? The answer, of course, was none. They would lock him in a cell and wait for him to 'fully and permanently recover from his mental incompetency.' They would have a long wait. Donald Lang was not a person who could be helped by electro-shock treatment or be reached in a group therapy session. He was unique and he needed highly specialized treatment if the wall that shut him off from the normal world was to be even slightly breached. But that was only Lowell Myers' opinion. The Court had dictated otherwise.

There is no ombudsman for the damned. The only way to alter the sentence imposed on his client was through the court system and no one knew this better than Lowell Myers. He filed a motion for a new trial, using as his sole argument the fact that he had not been permitted to be present during Dr. Myklebust's examination of Donald.

The motion was denied.

Lowell Myers then filed a Motion of Appeal and requested that the Court keep Donald confined in the Cook County Jail pending the outcome of that appeal.

That motion was denied and the order of the Court carried out. On 13 April 1966, Donald Lang was removed from the jail and taken to the State's maximum security hospital at Chester, Illinois, a small town overlooking the Mississippi River and the Missouri border. The hospital stood high above the river like a medieval grey stone fortress. It was far from Chicago, light years away from anything that Donald Lang had ever known before. There was no way for anyone to explain the reason he was being sent there, or for how long. The sense of total isolation that Donald must have felt when the gates of the hospital closed behind him can only be imagined with a feeling of horror.

Donald's brother, William—now referred to by all who knew him as Levi Yisrael—visited him several times at Chester. Each visit only increased his anger and dread. When he returned to Chicago he contacted Lowell Myers and told him what was happening to Donald.

'We've got to get him out of there. He's being beaten up and the men are using him. They're really doing a job on him!'

That Donald could be a target for perverts and sadists had been a nightmarish possibility. Donald could be used with impunity. Who could he complain to? Who would ever know? Chester, with its dungeon-like cells and granite walls was the worst possible place for Donald to be in, but there was no easy way of getting him out. Donald's only hope rested on his appeal, and the court that Myers appealed to was the Illinois Supreme Court.

The filing of an appeal with the Supreme Court is a lengthy and time-consuming project. The procedure is as formalized as a pavane, with no step out of place. The case history of the proceedings against Donald Lang beginning with his arrest for murder on 12 November 1965, up to the filing of a Motion with the Circuit Court for a new trial on 5 April 1966, had to be documented. The brief was bulky and complex but Myers felt that he was on solid ground in his assertion that the damaging

73

testimony of Dr. Myklebust should have been ruled as inadmissible evidence. Myers stated in his brief ...

In view of the Defendant's serious physical handicap, his attorney should have been given permission to be present at any examination conducted by a witness for the Prosecution.

The trial Court's refusal to permit this was in error. It made it impossible for the Defendant to defend himself and placed him at the mercy of the Prosecution.

The Judgment must be reversed and the case remanded for a new trial.

In addition, it is suggested that this is an appropriate time for the Court to consider the question of whether all defendants in sanity cases are entitled to the presence of their lawyers at examinations which are conducted by psychologists *who have been selected by the Prosecution.*

Since Donald could not talk to his lawyer, and tell his lawyer what had taken place at the competency examination, the lawyer was unable to make an effective cross-examination of the psychologist at the trial. The psychologist simply claimed that he *could not remember* what took place at the examination, and thus evaded any question that he did not like.

'Q. What was the next test that you gave him after the drawing test?

A. Well, I cannot give you a sequence of test by test for that afternoon. I don't think I could do it, even if I referred to the records.'

The psychologist would not have been able to get away with such evasive tactics if the lawyer had been permitted to be present at the examination, making his own notes of what actually took place.

Likewise, Donald could not speak to the jury and tell them what happened at the examination, he was entitled to have a witness present on his behalf.

This general subject was discussed by the U.S. Supreme Court in the *Miranda* case, where it was pointed out that the presence of the lawyer *as a witness* automatically curbs abuses and trickery.

The Prosecution says on page 10 of its Brief that we should not be given a new trial on the mental incompetency finding because Donald would still be *physically* incompetent to stand trial anyway.

Prosecution does not seem to understand the great difference between the two findings. If Donald is mentally O.K. but *physically* incompetent to stand trial (due to his deafmute handicap and his lack of knowledge of sign language) the result is that he *cannot* be put into a mental institution for the criminally insane.

We presume that the trial Court would then place him in a special school for deaf-mutes where he will be taught the sign language. When Donald has acquired a reasonable ability to communicate in sign language, he could then be placed on trial the same as anyone else. We believe that he would then be found not guilty, and if so, he would then go home and pick up the threads of his life where he left off.

The Prosecution is assuming that it *makes no difference* whether Donald is placed temporarily in a school to learn sign language; or whether he is placed permanently in a mental institution for the criminally insane for the rest of his life.

Of course it makes a difference!

Myers' Brief was meticulously put together and eloquently worded. It was submitted to the Illinois Supreme Court along with the Brief by the State's Attorney for the plaintiff-Appellee, the People of the State of Illinois, and assigned as docket number 40013. It would be the twenty-ninth day of March 1967, before the Appeal was ruled upon. Donald Lang had been in the mental hospital for nearly one year.

Justice Walter V. Schaefer delivered the opinion of the Court. Myers' contention that there should be a new trial because he had not been present during the mental testing of Donald Lang was not sustained. However, the Court ruled that Judge Napoli had erred in committing Donald to the Illinois Security Hospital at Chester. His authority had been only to place him in the hands of the Department of Mental Health. It was up to the Department to judge which of its institutions was best suited for a person of such multiple physical impairments.

Donald Lang was now free from incarceration as a lunatic. It was up to the Department of Mental Health to find a place where he could be kept while a serious attempt was made to teach him language skills so that, in time, he might stand trial on the charge of murder.

Lowell Myers talked over this partial victory with Donald's family. They were pleased that he was to be released from the mental institution and hoped that he could be placed in either the Dixon State School at Dixon, Illinois, or at the Lincoln State School near Peoria. Both institutions were minimum security training centres where the emphasis was on rehabilitation. Lowell Myers was pleased too, but he had hoped that the Supreme Court would have ruled on broader issues—namely the constitutionality of Chapter 38, Section 104 of the Illinois Revised Statutes. This revision of the Code of Criminal Procedures had been enacted in 1963 and its constitutionality had yet to be tested. It provided that a man could be put into a mental institution if he were charged with a criminal offence and found mentally incompetent to assist his lawyer in his defence. The Circuit Court had used this law to block Myers' motion that Donald Lang be placed on trial for the murder of Ernestine Williams. The State stressed in their Brief to the Supreme Court ...

> The Defendant complains that he was not permitted to go to trial on his murder indictment. At the time defendant made his demand for trial, he had been found physically incompetent to stand trial. A trial of one who is incompetent to stand trial violates due process of law. A defendant cannot waive the question of his incompetency to stand trial. By definition, one who is incompetent to stand trial is incompetent to waive his rights.
>
> Furthermore, at the time that trial was demanded by defendant, the Court had before it reports indicating that defendant was mentally incompetent to stand trial. Thus there was *bona fide* doubt of defendant's mental competency and the trial could not proceed with defendant's consent.

Section 104 was a neat trap—a Catch 22 of jurisprudence. It stated in a nutshell that even if the defendant were innocent he had no right to prove it, *because he was incompetent to stand trial*. Myers made an issue of this code in his Brief, mainly because the prosecution had raised the point, but also because he felt that the Donald Lang case might serve as a worthy challenge. Section 104 was, in his opinion, 'a very questionable

76

statute, and one that could easily be used to carry out great injustices.' But the Supreme Court had side-stepped the issue of Section 104 by simply ignoring its reference in Myers' Brief. Donald Lang was freed from the Illinois Security Hospital only because Judge Napoli had exceeded his authority in committing him there.

On 19 May 1967, Donald Lang was transferred by court order into the care of the Illinois Department of Mental Health and on 6 June 1967, was committed to the Dixon State School, in the lush farm country of Lee County, ninety miles from Chicago. He was closer to home, but he still had a long way to go.

CHAPTER VI

The Dixon State School had been founded in 1918 as both a home and a rehabilitation centre for mentally retarded children and young adults. It was in marked contrast to the maximum security facility at Chester. There were no stone walls at Dixon, only park-like grounds dotted with trees and shrubbery. This pastoral setting was dominated by the main buildings, imposing two-storied structures of red brick. The administration building, with its tall bell tower, was reminiscent of Independence Hall in Philadelphia. In architecture and landscaping, Dixon looked more like an Ivy League college than a state institution, but it was an institution and an overcrowded and understaffed one.

The range of Dixon's services had been expanded over the years to include not only the care and treatment of the mentally retarded, but all types of emotional and personality disorders as well. The effect was a population explosion. There were nearly four thousand inmates at the school when Donald Lang arrived there on the sixth of June.

Despite this serious overcrowding, the school was run with great efficiency and care. All new admissions had to go through a process of testing and diagnosis to determine what programmes they would be placed into, or whether they could be permitted to stay at Dixon at all. The testing of Donald Lang began on the afternoon of his arrival.

'My initial impression is that of a lonely, frustrated, young man with a total lack of ability to communicate.'

So wrote a therapist of the Speech and Hearing Department, the first entry in the Donald Lang casebook.

Aptitude tests of various kinds were given that first day, including tests for aphasia, receptive vocabulary, memory span, auditory discrimination and speech reading. Donald did poorly on all of the formal tests, just as he had done when tested by Dr. Myklebust at North-western, but the therapists at Dixon were not so quick to judge him.

'... It is the opinion of this examiner that Donald is a profoundly deaf man who has never developed sufficient language skills. He cannot be accurately tested at this time regarding potential to learn or perform due to his severe lack of expressive and receptive language skills. The question which appears to be paramount in this case is to determine his intellectual functioning level. His present functioning would appear to be rated at the severely to profoundly retarded level. However, it cannot be stated at this time how much of the retardation factor is due to cerebral dysgenesis and how much is directly related to the lack of language ability.'

Donald Lang was not automatically being ruled an imbecile because he grunted, made whining noises, couldn't copy the alphabet or put pegs into the proper holes. He would be tested again when he had become more adjusted to the Dixon routine and atmosphere. There was the distinct possibility, judging by his almost surly attitude during the tests, that he had deliberately done badly on the mechanical aptitude puzzles. Donald was a strong, physically healthy, twenty-two-year-old male. He had nothing but contempt for childish things—like wooden blocks and peg boards—but it would be several weeks before the therapists began to understand this aspect of his complex nature.

Donald was assigned to Cottage A-14, a large structure with twenty-two individual cell-like rooms. He was the only deaf-mute in the cottage but there were many young men living in it who were mentally handicapped. It was quickly discovered that Donald had only derision for these men whose abilities were less than his own.

He functioned well in the all male atmosphere of the cottage. He cooked breakfasts, swept floors and shined shoes, doing all of these tasks with an air of cheerful willingness. Work was an expression of his maleness. It was what he was used to. Mario Pullano had mentioned Donald's joy in working at the market, how he would glory in his ability to lift the heaviest sacks and take obvious pride in his speed at unloading trucks. This pride of maleness became more evident as Donald grew used to his surroundings. He would show off his strength by lifting other residents of the cottage, or by destroying soda pop cans in his bare hands. Outside of his occasional flashes of temper towards the mentally defective residents, he had adjusted well to life in the cottage and was considered nearly ready to take a more active part in the general community activities at Dixon.

There were still tests to be made however—a psychiatric examination and further tests on speech and hearing. The psychiatric staff at Dixon was limited to three qualified psychiatrists for three thousand residents, so it was obvious that psychiatric care would be limited to an almost cursory evaluation. Donald was examined a few days after his arrival at the school and again one month later. Both examinations were low key and informal. As all verbal communication was impossible, the psychiatrist was restricted to observing Donald's actions. The first thing he did was to show him a drawing—a man stabbing a woman with a knife. Donald reacted instantly, moving his hands wildly and making low, guttural sounds. The examiner took this to mean that he was attempting to explain the act and his part in it, that he was trying to say, 'Yes, I did it. I don't know why.' It was purely conjectural. Donald could also have been trying to say, 'Yes, I saw it, that was what happened—a man stabbed her with a knife.' His reaction to the simple drawing could be interpreted to mean almost anything.

After the various non-verbal intelligence tests were completed, the psychiatrist took Donald to the recreation centre, a large basement room walled with a wide assortment of athletic equipment and games. Nothing seemed strange to Donald. He slugged away at a punching bag, lifted barbells—choosing the heaviest set of weights—and accepted a challenge to play table tennis. He was good at the game, not only winning, but offering the doctor instruction on the proper way to hold his paddle.

There was an old piano in one corner of the room and the doctor gestured towards it. Donald pulled up a chair and sat down, rubbed his fingers as though trying to dry them and then began to press the keys. The psychiatrist wrote later in his report ...

'He started to press the keys with no exaggeration at all. At that moment, I asked him if he could hear; he turned around and signalled "yes". Both Mr. Brown and I, by signs, asked him if he could hear the tunes and the answer again was "yes". He seems to be perfectly aware of his surroundings and quite conscious of his movements and probably of his feelings.'

Could Donald Lang hear anything? Was he deaf, or was he suffering from aphasia or alexia? These two related brain disorders cause the loss of power to understand or repeat words. A person with visual, sensory, or optical alexia cannot recognize words. One with motor alexia understands words, but cannot say them. This, coupled with hearing loss, could have accounted for Donald's condition. Opinions differed. Donald was driven to the Speech and Hearing Clinic at Northern Illinois University, in nearby De Kalb, for evoked response audiometry tests. The diagnosis by Dr. Rose at De Kalb was similar to Dr. Myklebust's at North-western; that Donald suffered from profound sensori-neural hearing loss. Donald was also examined at Dixon by Dr. Joel Brumlik, a neurologist, and his observations were submitted to Dr. W. S. Rybak, assistant superintendent, psychiatric, at Dixon.

'During the examination, Donald was quite co-operative. Before the examination began, he was observed to speak to the security officers who accompanied him. This was voluntary. When there was some difficulty in adjusting the examining table, he smiled in a rather condescending manner, turned to one of the security officers and communicated, in a non-verbal fashion by talking behind his hand. He then made a gesture indicating that the examiner may be mentally disturbed! However, the patient was at no time bizarre. It was obvious that he was in contact with his environment enough to relate to it in a meaningful way. He seemed to understand what was required of him during the examination and co-operated, presumably by reading lips. At other times, he did not appear to understand and would shake his head to that effect. He was alert at all times and was willing to copy certain figures for the examiner. His figures were not complete, but it was the examiner's impression that this was more from boredom with the task than from any intrinsic lack of skill.

I can find no significant neurological findings to account for this patient's lack of verbal communication. I have reviewed the electroencephalogram and this confirms my impression. I have also reviewed Dr. Myklebust's findings. I do not believe that this boy is as mentally retarded as indicated by Dr. Myklebust's report, nor do I believe that his retardation is sufficient to account for his speech defect. There may be partial sensori-neural hearing loss, but I am more inclined to view the problem as aphasia.'

Opinions differed sharply as to the root cause of Donald's affliction, but all men agreed on one point—Donald Lang could not communicate. Could he be taught? That was the question uppermost in everyone's mind. No worthwhile attempt had ever been made, and Donald was now twenty-two, far beyond the optimum age for the training of deaf-mutes. But a way had to be found—or at least attempted.

Edward Mirus was an experienced teacher of the deaf. He had four deaf students in his speech therapy class at Dixon when Donald Lang was admitted. It would not overload his facilities, nor overtax his abilities, to admit one more. His first step was to make his own evaluation of Donald in order to see whether or not he was teachable.

Mirus spent three hours a day for six days with Donald, testing and observing him in an effort to guage his abilities and shortcomings. He became immediately aware of Donald's highly-developed perceptive powers and uncanny peripheral vision—attributes which had led many people to believe that Donald could hear. The teacher stood behind Donald's back, at an angle slightly greater than ninety degrees from a direct line of vision, and made an obscene gesture with his finger. Donald reacted with instant anger. Mirus then glanced towards an adjoining room and raised his eyebrows slightly. Donald shot him a questioning look and went to the room to see what was happening.

These simple 'tests' showed that Donald was keenly aware in a visual sense. This visual quickness formed a large part of his communications system. He could sense how people felt or what they wanted by studying their expressions or gestures. It was this perception that had made it easy for him to function on the loading docks. As for communicating his own wants or thoughts, Donald relied principally on gestures, 'explaining' at one point to Mirus that he had once operated a ferris wheel. The teacher was impressed by Donald's graphic pantomime, but he had doubts as to Donald's ability to deal with the abstracts of language. Donald could function on a primitive level by using his hands, but hands could merely express *things* —a ferris wheel, a coffee grinder, a truck. One could not express *tomorrow* or *last week* by a simple gesture. Donald had lived with *his* communication technique for twenty-two years. It would be very difficult for him to learn a new system, especially one as abstruse as the English language. It was not a matter of merely teaching him signs which would represent certain objects, but of trying to make him grasp the basic tools of language, that the letters C-A-T meant the animal, or that S-K-Y was that place where the S-U-N shone. To do this might take many years—if it could be done at all.

How intelligent was Donald Lang? There was no way for Mirus to judge. The summary of reports that he had read placed Donald anywhere from imbecile to average and, judging by what he had heard, the young man resented being tested with blocks, puzzles or mazes. Mirus tried another approach. He demonstrated the threading of a film strip projector and gestured for Donald to try it. Donald slipped the strip of film through the gate of the projector with no trouble at all. Mirus then showed him how to do a far more complicated task—the threading of a 16mm movie projector, a process that took several steps. Again Donald did it correctly the first time, a task that many perfectly normal people armed with an instruction manual from the manufacturer would have had trouble doing. Mirus did not know of Lowell Myers' experiment with the ballpoint pen, or that Donald could repair a fork lift truck or the gears on a bicycle, but it was immediately obvious to him that Donald showed a high aptitude for mechanically oriented material—a pattern of learning common to 'normal' deaf people.

In theory, Donald Lang appeared to be teachable. It was a process that could take a long time, but what were five or even ten years when weighed against the reward of language! Then Edward Mirus began to notice some disturbing facets to

Donald's personality that made the possibility of such teaching appear bleak.

'Donald *seems* to be willing to learn how to work with numbers, read and write. However, this may be a front. He may think that showing a willingness on his part to do things will give him more freedom than he has experienced in the past few months. As a result, he is very co-operative *with me*. Donald does not like to work in front of a group of people when he feels unsure of himself or when he feels he might fail and be ridiculed by the group. This was evidenced by his refusal to do academic work in front of the other deaf students. But, he was willing to work in front of myself and the cottage employee. He was able to outwardly tolerate correction of his mistakes by us. This may have been due to the fact that he respected us or was just co-operating to keep his gained freedom of three hours of class time at Tillman House.'

Mirus wrote these words in his report to Dr. Rybak, to be used in the staff meeting on Lang's case scheduled for mid-September. The inability of Donald to work within a group was a disturbing factor. The educational system at the State institution was not geared to a one-to-one teacher-pupil relationship. Donald's attitude was destructive to the small class. Not only would he refuse to work in front of the other deaf students, he would become angry if they made mistakes of any kind. When one student dropped an ashtray on the floor, Donald stormed out of the room. His tolerance level towards people who appeared 'dumb' was dangerously low.

'... Donald's world revolves about his attempts to prove that he is a man. He feels that the main proof of this is his strength which he likes to show off through rather overt actions such as smashing soda cans or lifting and man-handling people. If he is willing to learn, the materials presented to him must have an adult connotation. Instead of presenting number concepts as 1 ... 2 ... 3 ... through pictures of balls, boats, etc., they must be presented by means of money as 1¢ ... 5¢ ... 10¢. Letters of the alphabet must be presented through whole words such as his name instead of individual letters. In other words, the basic con-

84

cepts grasped by a child must be dressed up in an adult fashion, but yet presented simply. If not, Donald will feel insulted and will not co-operate in any way ...'

Mirus had no trouble in making Donald grasp the relationship between the printed signs 1¢ ... 5¢ ... etc., and the actual coins. Handed a dime, Donald would place it on the appropriate sign, but Mirus had no way of knowing that Donald had been taught to recognize various types of money very early in life. His father and his older brother had worked on this, as had Mario Pullano at the South Water Market. But Donald's concept of signs seemed to end there.

'... During the six days, Donald did not accept signs as a means of communication. I feel that he realizes "normal", that is *hearing* people use speech as their main means of communication. Since he strives to be normal, Donald uses vocalizations with mouth movements in an attempt to communicate. His vocal rhythm and rhythm of facial gestures would seem to indicate that he had hearing, but his vocalizations refute this. This is another example of his perceptual power. I feel that I could get Donald to use signs, but it would take a long period of time to do so.'

And under conditions that were not possible at Dixon unless Donald could learn to work within a group.

On 13 September 1967, Donald was taken from his cottage by one of the social workers and escorted to the main administration building where the all-important staff meeting was to take place. It was the procedure at Dixon for all inmates to be staffed within a few months of their arrival. The conclusions reached at the staffing would determine the inmate's future course of treatment. There were seventeen people in the room when Donald was led into it. Some were familiar to him—Mr. Mirus, the teacher of the deaf, and Mr. Brown, the aide in charge of Cottage A-14—but most of the men and women seated at the long conference table were strangers. They included Dr. Rybak, several speech and hearing specialists, a clinical psychologist, three registered nurses and various recreation workers and therapists.

The record states that Donald was quiet and subdued during the course of the meeting. There was no way that he could have known the purpose for his being there, and he must have felt some sense of foreboding. The people seated at the table had the appearance of a jury.

Mr. Atkins, a unit director at Dixon, led off the proceedings by reading the background information they had on Donald. This included material furnished by the Cook County Mental Health Clinic and by Dr. Haines at the Behaviour Clinic. The documentation was thorough, from birth to commitment at Chester. Reduced to one and a half pages of typewritten copy, Donald's life was a depressing chronicle.

It was all there, read by Mr. Atkins to sixteen interested and attentive people. Donald's fall from his crib ... Donald at two-and-a-half being turned down by the Parkman Deaf Oral School for losing control of his bowels ... Donald at thirteen breaking his hand, kicking nurses and refusing to take his medicine ... Donald stealing a truck and being sent to the Jacksonville State Hospital, a mental institution, for observation ... Donald indicted for murder and the resultant competency hearings. '... Judgment was entered on the findings of mental incompetency and he was admitted to Illinois Security Hospital 13 April 1966, and brought here to Dixon on 6 June of this year.'

Mr. Basile, director of Unit V—the section in which Donald had been placed—then asked: 'Was that his only problem, deafness?'

'That and the investigation of the possible theft,' Atkins replied. 'At least, that's the only thing recorded here.'

'He was admitted to mental hospitals on several occasions,' Dr. Rybak added. 'He was in Psychopathic Hospital ... Kanakee State and Jacksonville State—probably because of deafness. He was unable to communicate with anyone and they felt he would stay this way so they put him in a mental hospital. There was a type of behaviour problem, too; maybe classified as a social or dyssocial [sic], something like that.'

'Was he granted an absolute discharge from Jacksonville?' Basile asked.

Atkins glanced down at the dossier in front of him. 'Yes. They tried to get him admitted to the deaf school there but the school wouldn't accept him because of his behaviour. He was a management problem inasmuch as he attempted to escape

86

from the hospital on numerous occasions. He was given an absolute discharge, without psychosis.'

Mr. F. N. Gorham, supervisor of the Speech and Hearing Department, then asked : 'There seems to be no real reason for his deafness indicated except for the fall from the crib—which I doubt. Was there nothing other than that?'

'No.'

There was, but Mr. Atkins had never seen it. In researching the medical background of Donald Lang for the court, Dr. Haines of the Cook County Behaviour Clinic had uncovered a scrap of information that had gone overlooked. At the age of five weeks, Donald had contracted a severe case of chickenpox and had spent seven days in a hospital. Chickenpox, or varicella, is a virus infection that is both rare and dangerous in a child that young. Fever and infection could possibly have caused deterioration of certain cranial nerves, including the acoustic. There was also the possibility that Donald's case had been misdiagnosed. Spotted fever, or spinal meningitis as it is now called, has similar symptoms, including fever and rash. Without a spinal tap, this insidious disease cannot be diagnosed. Had a spinal tap been performed on the five-week-old Donald Lang? The record does not say. If Donald had had meningitis as a baby, even a mild form, the damage to cranial nerves could have been extensive—and permanent.

Why Donald had become deaf was an academic question to the staff. Dixon was not a hospital, it was a dumping ground for the misborn and the unwanted. Its nearly four thousand young inmates were society's rejects. Birth or environment had inflicted traumas that made them incapable of living independent lives. They were mongoloids and schizoids, the emotionally disturbed and the mentally incompetent. Dixon's only function was to take care of these people and to try, if at all possible, to train them for some kind of role in a complex and competitive world.

Mr. F. N. Barber of the Speech and Hearing Department then read his report on Donald to the staff.

'It is the opinion of this examiner that Donald is a profoundly deaf man who has never developed sufficient language skills. He cannot be accurately tested at this time regarding potential to learn or perform due to his severe lack of expressive and receptive language skills. However, it might be assumed that with careful instruction, provided through gestures, he

87

could learn to perform meaningful tasks. His speech, or more specifically, his oral attempts, resemble those of a profoundly deaf child who has never heard speech well enough to develop verbal communication. His graphic skills are completely inadequate for expression. Although he is able to copy single letters and words of three or four letters, he demonstrated total inability to print or write any comprehensible words spontaneously. Receptively, he demonstrated no understanding of any of the printed words presented to him. Due to his age, present frustration level, and the above-mentioned information, the prognosis for speech development is extremely poor.'

Edward Mirus gave his report on the six days he had spent with Donald in the Speech and Hearing Clinic. He told of Donald's mechanical aptitude and highly-developed perception. He told also of Donald's impatience and his difficulty in working within a group. But he did not dismiss him as a hopeless case. In six days of observing Donald, he had gained some insight into his personality.

'I would say Donald's performance ability would probably be close to normal. His seeming retardation could be attributed to his deafness and from the environment which he comes from in Chicago. I would not try to guess at his verbal ability because there is no effective means of communication. I would recommend that he be tested with the Leiter or the Nebraska test of learning aptitudes which are non-verbal intelligence tests for the deaf. However, it is very important that the examiner gain rapport and an acquaintance with Donald before testing him or no results will be obtained.'

'Dr. F. N. Tovar did a psychiatric evaluation on him,' Dr. Rybak said. 'In summary, Dr. Tovar made the diagnosis ... "Emotionally unstable personality." The patient impressed Dr. Tovar as being able to distinguish between right and wrong but at the same time act upon strong impulse, if provoked. How has he been in the cottage, Mr. Brown?'

'He's behaved very well and co-operated with us very well.'

'Has he ever been provoked?'

'Yes,' Brown said. 'We had him provoked when he wouldn't come out of his room one morning. He showed anger, but without problems.'

'We've teased him quite a bit,' Basile said, 'so have the residents on the cottage. I've never seen him attack or show real anger towards anyone.'

Dr. Rybak nodded. 'Okay, but he is in a situation where he knows he has to control himself and so he will control himself.'

'Is it definite that he killed this woman?' one of the therapists asked.

'I don't know,' Dr. Rybak replied. 'The police are convinced that he did, and they have evidence. His lawyer indicated that he could show evidence that he didn't kill her, but every defence will indicate that, so I really don't know.'

'He'd like to return to Chicago,' Atkins said. 'Ed told me about that ferris wheel business and I sat down with Donald for about an hour. He showed me how he used to work the wheel, you know, through gestures, and then he pointed in the direction of the gate and then at the clock, indicating that it was time to go to work.'

'What has he been doing on the cottage all day?' Rybak asked.

'Going to school in the afternoon,' Brown said, 'and we work him quite a bit in the morning.'

'I brought along some drawings that Donald did in class,' Mirus said. 'We were working on printing. I would print his name and have him reproduce it. As you can see, he can copy but he can't do anything on his own. After showing how to work the movie projector, he was real enthused and this drawing is supposed to be a projector. And these are some scribblings he did the other day. He worked at it beautifully. Just to look at him, standing, the way he carries himself, he looks like a normal person. It's when he opens his mouth and tries to communicate that you know there's something wrong with him.'

'I hope I didn't give the impression in my report that I think Donald is basically retarded,' Mr. Barber said. 'What I was attempting to point out was, that if he were just to be observed trying to communicate, his performance would be comparable to that of a retarded person. Now, as far as his ability to learn, I'm not in any position to comment at all. But I definitely feel he has potential.'

'What I was talking about was the *non-verbal* level,' Mirus said. 'When he works with *things*, he is just about normal.'

Donald did not appear to be normal. He sat staring at the wall, almost as though he were catatonic. Mirus felt it necessary to explain this to the panel.

'In a group like this, he'll stare blankly ahead. In class with the other kids he wouldn't do anything, wouldn't participate, he just sat staring ahead.'

'If I stood up he would notice it,' Barber remarked.

'That's true,' Dr. Rybak said. 'His sense of "feel" is much greater when he stares at one point. He can actually see much more this way because his peripheral field is greater.'

Everyone at the long table stared at Donald Lang and Donald Lang stared at the wall.

'What exactly are we after?' a therapist asked. 'We all accept the fact that he's deaf. Are we concerned mainly with how normal he is?'

'Yes,' Rybak replied. 'He's deaf, there's no question about that. We are trying to find out what we can recommend from the psychological and psychiatric point of view. Can he stand trial or not? Should he be outside or stay in an institution?'

Opinions came quickly from all sides of the table.

'He's definitely not able, at this time anyway, to defend himself or understand the charges against him.'

'I think he can understand, but he can't defend himself.'

'I don't think he can understand what the charges are.'

'He understands right from wrong—according to Dr. Tovar.'

'If he saw a picture of a female being stabbed, would he comprehend?'

'Dr. Tovar did that. He showed him a drawing of a man killing a woman.'

'How did he react?'

'He shook his head like he understood.'

'We all do things in anger and are sorry for them later.'

'Either this particular act occurred two years ago or it didn't. Was there provocation or not? This is what concerns some of us. Is further training going to help Donald grasp what the trial is all about? Can we do anything further so that at least he will have a better understanding of the trial?'

That question hinged on Donald's personality. No one believed that he was an imbecile. In fact, it was the consensus that he was bright, but would he submit to the ordeal of teaching?

'He shows a definite refusal to co-operate,' Barber said. 'If you induce him to co-operate and he reaches the point where he cannot continue, he refuses and it's almost impossible to get him going again. He reaches a particular point, then goes no further. He goes so far as to refuse to even look at you. He'll throw papers across the desk, throw pencils, shove things away. There is complete refusal.'

'He was very hostile to me the first day,' Edward Mirus stated. 'Then I showed him how to work the movie projector and we went to the Tillman House and had coffee—he made the coffee by the way. The second time I saw him, he warmed up a bit more and the third day, he started to laugh when the others laughed. Just yesterday, he joined in the class, and he will actually smile at me now. The problem is that he's going to be in a class with four other kids and he needs individual attention. If I try to focus all my attention on Donald, I will have to slide the other four. The way the classes are now, it is hard to set up on a one-to-one basis.'

'Okay,' Dr. Rybak said, 'let me summarize this. We all agree that Donald is suffering from total deafness of sensori-neural origin. Now, as to psychiatric diagnosis, I would say that he has a passive-aggressive personality, aggressive type. He is able to understand and use very simple gestures as a means of communication. He never developed adequate sign language for meaningful communication. He is able to respond to directions by gestures and is able to accept authority. He is able to understand between right and wrong on a basic, primitive level but is unable to communicate this understanding. He is unable to stand trial on the grounds of inability to communicate and perceive abstract ideas. It is my recommendation that Donald continue deaf education classes to emphasize sign language development. He will have to remain in the security cottage under close supervision as he is emotionally able to respond in a violent manner to external and internal stresses. The prognosis for Donald Lang is this: Poor for learning communication. Possible learning of simple skills, but probably will be in need of constant supervision.'

Copies of the minutes of this meeting were sent to the two men who had the greatest interest in Donald's progress—Lowell Myers and Jerome F. Goldberg, Special Counsel to the Director of the Department of Mental Health in Chicago. It was Goldberg's duty to inform the court when Donald Lang became competent to stand trial. Judging by the staff report it would be a long time before he could do so.

CHAPTER VII

Cottage A-14 was officially designated as an I.T.U. closed ward. In layman's language, this meant that the cottage was part of the Intensive Therapy Unit and that it contained cell-like rooms with doors that could be shut—and locked. There were no punishment cells at Dixon, nor guards with clubs. It was a school, not a prison, and discipline was enforced on a parent-child level. Punishment for the unruly was banishment to one's room for a few hours, or the loss of special privileges. There were twenty-one inmates living in Cottage A-14, which was in marked contrast to the sixty or more sleeping in the regular dormitories where there were no individual rooms, only steel frame beds lined side by side in three long rows. The more difficult cases were assigned to A-14, and although there were numbers of mentally retarded or emotionally disturbed people in the wards, the most profoundly retarded or disturbed were in A-14. Donald Lang was also there, initially for observation, but as time went on, many of the aides and directors at the school became convinced that he would probably have to stay there on a permanent basis.

Donald was in a situation over which he had no control and could voice no objection. The psychiatric examinations of Donald had been shallow. He could not lie on a couch and tell the psychiatrist the story of his life, and no member of his family had come to Dixon to offer any insight into the complexities of his personality. So Donald was weighed and judged strictly by his day-to-day behaviour, and that behaviour was erratic and sometimes violent.

He had never functioned well in confinement. The pattern of his upbringing had been one of great freedom. His mother, possibly blaming herself in some way for her son's affliction, had pampered him. Donald as a boy had been able to do things, and get away with things that would have been impossible for his brothers and sister. He could wander away from home for hours or days at a time and come back without fear of punishment. It would have been unthinkable to spank Donny, to punish a child so terribly punished already. Donald grew up taking this freedom for granted. When travelling carnivals came to the West Side, he would run off with them, to operate the ferris wheel or do other odd jobs—not for money, but for the pure joy of being at the centre of whirling gears and brightly-coloured cars. He could not have heard the hurdy-gurdy, but he would have felt its vibrations and sensed the laughter and the screaming of the crowds. The carnival atmosphere of the South Water Market had held an even greater fascination for him. He had proved his manhood there by doing a man's work for a man's pay. His freedom of movement had been absolute. There had been no time clock for him to punch. He came when he wanted to and left when he wanted to.

Donald's reaction to previous confinement was a matter of record. It began with the first threat to his cherished freedom of movement at the age of thirteen when he had broken his hand and had been packed off by the hospital authorities to a mental clinic. Years later, when he had been sent to Jacksonville State Hospital for observation because of the truck-stealing incident, the records again showed that Donald's reaction had been one of violent rebellion. His behaviour at that time had been so intractable that he had been judged unfit to attend the deaf school at that mental institution.

Now, he was confined at Dixon in an I.T.U. cottage, and his feelings of frustration were drawn to the snapping point.

By late November 1967, several incidents had been reported to Dr. Rybak by the cottage aides and supervisors. Donald's aggression towards the mentally retarded inmates of Cottage A-14 was of grave concern, as was his behaviour in Mr. Mirus' class. Donald spent his afternoons in the deaf class, but did not appear to be making any noticeable progress. The only bright spot in Donald's adjustments to the school seemed to be taking place during the mornings when the cottage aides put him to work. He would do any task, cheerfully and willingly, from cleaning his own room to washing the cottage windows. Donald had arrived at Dixon without any money and none had been sent by his family. This lack of funds prevented him from buying any luxury items from the school's canteen. He liked to smoke, but the only way he could do so was by bumming cigarettes from others. One of the cottage aides took it upon himself to reward Donald for his work by giving him a dollar a week so that he could at least buy himself a couple of packs of cigarettes. Instead of being grateful for this pocket money, Donald became abusive and demanded more. This incident was duly reported to Dr. Rybak.

Early in December, Donald's family contacted Lowell Myers and inquired if it were possible for Donald to be granted a pass so that he could come home for a few days, possibly around Christmas. The issuance of home passes was a common enough procedure at Dixon, and Lowell Myers passed on the family's request to Jerome Goldberg at the Mental Health Office in Chicago. On 7 December Mr. Goldberg received a two-page letter from Dr. Rybak explaining why such a pass was not possible. The letter stated, in part:

'... Repeatedly, Donald has demonstrated disgust (in a physical, abusive manner) at those residents of the cottage with lesser ability than himself. Our concern became greater when he extended this type of behaviour in the classroom situation. He became less tolerant of the deaf educator's instructions and here again would slap those residents in the class for not grasping the intended concepts as quickly as he felt they should. At this point, it was necessary to return him to the Intensive Therapy Unit in hopes that he would imply from our actions that his behaviour was not acceptable.

Because Donald had no money of his own, the unit director obtained a dollar on a weekly basis so that Donald might have cigarettes. Rather than being satisfied with this expression of empathy, he demanded more.

Finally, when he left the cottage in an apparent attempt to run off, we isolated him on the Intensive Therapy Unit where he now remains.

It is for the above reasons and the seriousness of the charges against him that the home visit request may not be granted.'

A copy of this letter was sent to Myers who set about drafting a letter of his own. He felt that it was important for Dr. Rybak, and all of the other top officials of the Dixon School, to understand completely the extraordinary legal process that had placed Donald in their care. He was, Myers pointed out, very special. He wrote:

'Donald's Commitment is Neither Civil Nor Criminal. *He Has a Special Status.*

A civil commitment statute usually provides that if a person cannot take care of himself, or if he would be a danger to himself or others, then he can be committed until such time as he is able to take care of himself. I would suppose that almost everyone committed to Dixon was committed under such a statute, after due proof that they cannot take care of themselves.

This is not true of Donald. In Donald's case, it was fully *admitted* at his trial that he is fully able to work and support himself without any difficulty. That was not the issue.

Donald was tried under an entirely different statute (first enacted in 1963) which said that if a person is *charged* with a crime and he is incompetent *to stand trial*, then he shall be committed to the Department. This statute provides that the defendant is NOT ALLOWED to stand trial, even if he has a hundred independent witnesses to prove that he is innocent; and even if he is *demanding* to be put on trial—so that he can prove that he is innocent. This statute says the defendant is *not permitted* to prove that he is innocent of the criminal charge.

There are serious doubts whether this special statute is constitutional. The U.S. Supreme Court in the case of Lynch v. Overholser, 1962, 369 U.S. 705 strongly hinted that they thought such statutes were unconstitutional, if they are used to stop a defendant from getting a criminal trial which he desires to have.

In Donald's case the jury found that Donald is both physically and mentally incompetent *to stand trial*. Donald seems to have a total block for language (aphasia). This could be considered either physical (together with deafness) or mental.

As you know, aphasia does not necessarily affect a person's general ability. A man can have severe aphasia and be totally unable to communicate—and still work, support a family, and lead a useful and satisfying life. That is what Donald was doing prior to this matter. He was working, making a living, was a member of the local YMCA and was living a quiet and useful life.

The Legal Duty of Your Department

Under the Court Order in this case (entered by Judge Powers) your Department is supposed to give Donald treatment that will make him competent to stand trial. In other words, the Department is supposed to teach him to communicate. I understand that you are now working on this.

The fact that Donald has been found incompetent to stand trial does not mean that he has been found incompetent in any other manner. In fact, there is a legal presumption that he is competent in all other respects.

Donald would be perfectly free to go back to work and to study language in the evenings, or some other arrangement worked out, subject to the approval of your Department.

You can see from the above that Donald's position *is* quite different from that of others who have been found mentally incompetent *to take care of themselves.*

Donald's Attitude at Dixon

In your letter . . . you point out that Donald has been irritated at Dixon by some of the retarded people that he is put with. There is nothing unusual about that. I think many of the nurses and doctors also get irritated with some of the retarded patients.

You mention that Donald had tried to go home on one occasion. There are quite a few lawyers who would testify that his present commitment is illegal. Indeed, the Supreme Court might very well say so. I do not see anything unusual about his wanting to go home.

You say that Donald was not satisfied with the one dollar a week that was given to him. Donald's work is worth about a hundred dollars per week—and Donald is well aware of it—because he has worked and supported himself for many years. He may feel that one dollar per week is underpayment for the work that he is actually doing at Dixon. I understand that he is doing a considerable amount of work there.

I should think that if Donald goes home for a visit, the irritations at Dixon will be left behind him and will not exist at his home. (There are no retarded people at his home.)

The fact that Donald gets irritated at Dixon is no reason

to stop him from going home where he will not be subject to those irritations.

Donald's Behaviour at Home

Most of the patients at Dixon could not get along on the outside. They were committed for that reason, after due proof that they could not take care of themselves.

Donald's case is just the opposite. He always got along fine at home. There was *never* any claim of any kind, by anyone that he cannot get along on the outside. We must keep in mind that his commitment is *only* because he cannot stand trial due to his lack of communication ability. This is a different matter.

The Question to be Decided at This Time

The immediate question is whether Donald should be given a home visit at this time.

From the legal standpoint, I think your Department should not deny him that right unless it would *stop* him from learning to communicate. (The Department's *sole* responsibility is to teach him to communicate.)

The Department's role is not that of a custodian (which is the usual situation). It is acting more in the role of a school teacher. The fact that a student may not be doing too well in his studies in school—does not give the school the right to stop the student from going home. He has a right to go home, regardless of his progress in his studies.

I would appreciate it, if you would give this matter your thoughtful consideration (in view of the unusual nature of this situation) and perhaps obtain legal advice on the matter; and then kindly write to me.'

The letter clarified Donald's peculiar legal position, and it offered some insight into the reason for Donald's anger at receiving a dollar a week for his labour, but other than that it had no effect. Donald did not get a pass to go home and he was not removed completely from the I.T.U. cottage. However, an effort was made to make his family aware that he needed pocket money, and if it were not possible for Donald to visit them in Chicago, they were welcome to visit him at Dixon.

James Basile, Director of Unit V (the I.T.U. unit), contacted Donald's brother William, and began a brief correspondence with him. William sent some cheques, but they had been made out to Julia Lang, dead since 1965, and had never been endorsed by her.

'We are returning the cheques which you sent us,' Mr. Basile wrote on 29 January 1968. 'Since they are not endorsed by Julia Lang, we cannot cash them. Furthermore, due to the dates, we are doubtful they can be cashed. We would appreciate having some contact with Donald's relatives. Since we cannot communicate with him, it is difficult to know his wishes. From his actions and signs, we know that he is asking for his relatives to come and see him. When the other boys on the cottage have company, Donald's desire to see his family becomes greater. He does not understand why he does not have company.'

A log sheet was kept on each inmate at Dixon, noting anything that was important or out of the ordinary. There was such a log kept on Donald Lang, and by reading it one gets a brief, tantalizing view of his life there. It is like looking at a movie screen on which flicker brief images of shadow and light.

19-12-67 Donald Lang striking other residents. Placed in his room on I.T.U. at 1.00 p.m.

3-2-68 Donald Lang's brother and cousins visited him on the cottage. Donald's cousin took it upon himself to tell John Davis, another resident on A-14, his grandmother had passed away last week and was buried on Friday. It was not felt that this was the proper way to break the news to John. Also, Donald's brother tried to give the aides a bad time.

27-3-68 Brad Mitchell struck Donald Lang in the nose with his fist for apparently no reason at 7.30 a.m.; no injuries visible at this time.

4-6-68 Donald Lang released to open side at 9.45 a.m.

12-7-68 Donald Lang complains that he has a finger that hurts him. Some of the other residents stated that he hurt himself yesterday while horseback riding at White Pines stable. Was sent to A-dispensary for X-ray.

4-10-68 At 6.30 a.m., Donald Lang was fighting Maurice and did something with his glasses. Lang's lock box was taken to the office. Maurice's glasses were found in Donald's lock box. Donald has used Maurice for sodomy purposes.

98

13-10-68   During the 11 to 7 shift, Donald Lang had been let out of his closed room to go to the restroom. Just then, Lorenzo Ragatham tried to strangle Mr. Hopper and Donald helped Mr. Hopper get free of Ragatham.

9-11-68   Donald Lang went bowling with another resident and an employee. Donald Lang on a date to the movie.

Donald's life during this period is a strange blend of the idyllic and the macabre—Donald goes horseback riding or bowling—Donald saves a man from being strangled. Donald sodomizes a friend. Donald on a date to the movie. In the context of the school itself, none of these events are strange or paradoxical. The special privileges for good behaviour included trips into the town of Dixon, population 20,000, where the loosely supervised inmates could go bowling, see a movie, or utilize any other recreational facilities that the small town had to offer. But these breaks were rare. For the most part, life at the school was an unchanging and monotonous routine in a grossly overcrowded environment. There were girls at Dixon, but they were carefully separated from the boys, and there is little doubt that sexual tension played a part in Donald's frustrations. His sexual pattern had been formed by observing the truck drivers and the whores at the South Water Market. He had not observed love, merely an exchange of money for a brief physical act. His method of getting a woman for himself had been primitive—he would reach beneath her skirt and hold out a five dollar bill. He attempted a variation of this method several times at Dixon with girls he came in contact with during various therapy sessions. He did not hold up any money, but he made his wants known by touching the girls between the legs. These advances were not well received, to put it mildly, and usually resulted in Donald's being removed from the class and sent back to the cottage for confinement in his room. His use of another boy for sexual purposes was not construed as blatant homosexuality on Donald's part. Such incidents were as common at Dixon as they would have been in any other institution where large numbers of young, virile men lived in circumstances of enforced celibacy.

In order to keep Donald from disturbing the girls, he was placed in work therapy groups that were all male. It was hoped

99

that separating him from females would lessen his tensions and feelings of frustration. This manoeuvre seemed to be effective judging by the log sheets. Fewer incidents of anti-social behaviour were recorded after this move took place.

Donald thrived in the masculine atmosphere of his shop classes. He was a hard worker and quickly grasped the fundamentals of woodworking and metal shaping. The work therapy shops at Dixon were geared to making utilitarian objects, such as knives, spoons, wooden bowls and table legs which could be sold to the public, so the work standards were kept high. Donald was considered the best worker at Dixon by the shop foremen.

Edward Mirus could not say the same. Donald's progress in the deaf class had come to a complete standstill. He could not, or would not, learn and his behaviour has disintegrated to the point where his mere presence in the class was destructive to the progress of the other students. Mirus was reluctant to admit failure, but by April of 1969 it was painfully obvious to him that Donald would never learn to communicate in any meaningful way. His grasp of basic sign language was no greater than it had been when Mirus had first tested him. He reported this to David Edelson, Superintendent of the Dixon School.

Edelson realized the implications of Mirus' report. Donald had been sent to the school for one reason and one reason only —to be taught how to communicate. If that was judged to be impossible, there seemed to be no reason for keeping him there. On 2 May 1969, he sent this letter to Jerome Goldberg in Chicago :

'... Based on our experience with Donald Lang, it appears that he will never acquire the necessary communication skills needed to participate and co-operate at his trial. He has rejected all of our efforts to instruct him and has refused to participate and co-operate with his instructor. The probability for his acquiring the necessary communication skills at any future date is unlikely. However, it is our impression that Donald is functioning at a nearly normal level of performance in areas other than communication. He is capable of fairly complex operations and tasks which would tend to support our opinions concerning his overall abilities.

Since Donald's commitment to the Department of Mental Health is based on physical and mental incompetence and the probability of appropriate functioning in the former (sic) area is doubtful, it would be our suggestion that you contact Donald's lawyer in order that appropriate legal action be initiated. Reviewing his lawyer's correspondence, it would seem that if his case came to court, sufficient evidence could be produced which would clear him of all charges.

It is apparent now that Donald's future must be decided in a court of law. He will not be able to communicate even in the limited sense we had at first anticipated ...'

Lowell Myers received a copy of this letter. He was disappointed but not unduly surprised by its contents. The chances for such learning had been slim in view of Donald's educational background. He was twenty years too late for school.

The letter did not solve Donald's predicament, however. The school had given up on him, but he was still bound there by the law. For Edelson to say that Donald's future must now be decided in court was well and good, but the question was— could Donald be brought into court? Myers decided to try.

On 29 August 1969, Myers filed a petition for a Writ of habeas corpus in the Circuit Court of Cook County, demanding that Donald Lang be released from the custody of the Mental Health Department and brought before the court, there to be either dismissed, or placed on trial for the murder of Ernestine Williams. The Great Writ of habeas corpus is the cornerstone of Anglo-Saxon law. Of all the guarantees wrested from King John by the English barons in 1215, habeas corpus was the most important. It provided that no man could be deprived of his personal freedom without due process of law. It virtually eliminated, in the English-speaking world at least, the mediaeval custom of locking a man away in a dungeon without trial. Habeas corpus—you (shall) have the body—show us the man you are holding so that his peers may judge him. Lowell Myers was now asking the court to produce the 'body' of Donald Lang.

'... Donald Lang is now being held by the Illinois Department of Mental Health ... and he is imprisoned.'

So began Lowell Myers' petition on behalf of his client. He detailed the various manoeuvres that had sent Donald to the Dixon School, and he outlined the reasons why that commitment was now wrong ...

'... It may have been proper for Donald Lang to be kept in custody for two years while the Department of Mental Health made a bona fide attempt to teach him to communicate. If that attempt had succeeded, he could then have been placed on trial in the usual manner and the problem would have been solved. However, the attempt to teach him to communicate has failed. We are now faced with the basic constitutional question of whether a man can be imprisoned forever because he cannot communicate and because he is merely accused of a crime. The answer is, of course, that a man cannot be imprisoned forever for those reasons.

Although the original imprisonment at Dixon State School may have been lawful, because it was for a reasonable purpose ... that reason has now expired and no longer exists ...

To keep Donald Lang in custody at this time, and forever, is a violation of his constitutional rights as guaranteed to him ... by the 4th, 5th, 6th, 7th, 8th, and 14th amendments of the United States Constitution ...

I request this Honourable Court to issue the GREAT WRIT OF HABEAS CORPUS directed to the Director of the Department of Mental Health of the State of Illinois, commanding him to produce Donald Lang before the Bar of this court ...

And, if the State's Attorney of Cook County, Illinois then wishes to proceed with the criminal trial of that charge, then Donald Lang will not oppose that. On the contrary, Donald Lang wishes to be placed on trial so that he can prove that he is innocent and go home ...'

This petition was considered carefully by Judge Powers of the Circuit Court and on 9 September 1969, he handed down his opinion ...

Petition for Writ of habeas corpus—denied.

CHAPTER VIII

Lost causes can be lonely. Lowell Myers was alone in the struggle to free Donald Lang. The plight of an illiterate, black deafmute seemed of little importance in a year of history-making events. Nineteen sixty-nine was the year man first walked on the moon. It was the year the 'Chicago Seven' went to trial; a United States Supreme Court Justice resigned under public pressure; a small island in Massachusetts called Chappaquiddick was on everybody's lips. The denial of a writ of habeas corpus for Donald Lang did not make the newspapers. Even Donald's family was strangely silent. As Lowell Myers began the laborious process of filing an appeal in the Illinois Supreme Court, he received a letter from Dixon ...

'... We are writing to you for assistance in contacting members of Donald Lang's family.

It has been nearly a year since Donald has heard from anyone. He has heard nothing from his (step) mother. Is she deceased? He often becomes quite disturbed because of this loss of contact with the family ...'

There was little that Myers could do about *that*. The process of filing an appeal with the Supreme Court had not become any less difficult and time consuming than it had been in 1966 when Myers had first approached them for a decision on Donald. He was asking now that the high court reverse the decision of the circuit court in denying his writ of habeas corpus. To do this involved a great deal of research in an attempt to find precedents that would apply to Donald's case. Myers could feel for Donald's misery, but he held a growing confidence that his ordeal would soon be over. Research had revealed an interesting case which was uncannily similar to Donald's. This was *Regina v. Roberts* and it had taken place in England in 1953.

The defendant, Roberts, was a deaf-mute with a total lack of communication skills. A criminal charge had been filed against him, but the Counsel for the Crown claimed that he could not be given a trial because he was—echoes of Donald Lang—'... incapable of understanding the nature of the proceedings.' The Queen's Counsel wished the defendant to be placed in Broadmoor Mental Hospital '... until Her Majesty's pleasure be made known.' A polite way of saying 'for ever'.

Roberts' barrister wanted his client to stand trial because he felt that the Crown had no case against him. There were no precedents in English law for the Court to go by, so it broke new ground by declaring that Roberts must stand trial because if he did not '... it might result in the grave injustice of detaining as a criminal lunatic a man who was in actuality innocent.'

The Court had more to say ...

'... the defence might wish to tender a witness who, if he was believed, could prove that the defendant was ten miles away at the time of the crime. It cannot, I think, be our law that, by some formality of procedure, counsel for the defendant should be prevented from laying matters of that sort before the jury, and so achieving for his client, if he can, a verdict of not guilty.'

Roberts had his trial and the jury found him not guilty. The Crown's case against him had been virtually non-existent, and yet if the English Court had not ruled that he was entitled to a trial, he would have been placed in a mental hospital and kept there until the day he died!

Donald Lang v. The Department of Mental Health of the State of Illinois would be the first case of its kind to come up in the United States. As such, any foreign ruling might be applicable to show precedent. *Regina v. Roberts* fitted the bill and Myers worked the details into his brief.

The laws of the United States are not carved in stone. They are supple chains with new links being forged every day. These links are the decisions handed down by the various court systems. A skilful lawyer takes these decisions and uses them to build his argument, link by thoughtful link. Lowell Myers was doing just that, reading through countless volumes of trial records to find those precedent-setting cases that might have a bearing on various points of law, or on Donald's constitutional rights. It was a painstaking task, but by the closing months of 1969, the cases had begun to pile up ... *Hernandez v. Texas* ... *Klopfer v. North Carolina* ... *Duncan v. Louisiana* ... *Truax v. Raich* ... *Pointer v. Texas* ... *Kent v. Dulles* ... *Robinson v. California* ...

Myers' brief was taking shape. It was nearly ready for submission.

At Dixon State School life went on. Donald Lang continued attending the deaf class, but it was a mere formality. Edward Mirus was not reaching him and Donald was becoming increasingly fretful and bored. He was cutting class a good deal and leaving the school grounds, not to run away, but to go bowling in town. Donald's performance in the workshops had not suffered, however. He was still thought of as one of the best workers, conscientious and reliable. He had the sympathy and goodwill of almost all of the aides, therapists and unit directors at the school and, in the upper echelons, even more active support. Both Dr. Rybak and David Edelson were considering plans to actively help Donald when, or if, he should go to court. It was suggested at a staff meeting that the school prepare a letter formally recommending that, in the opinion of all concerned, Donald Lang posed no threat to the community and that all charges against him be dropped. This plan ran into a serious snag by a minor but disturbing incident which took place in one of Donald's work groups.

Donald was an object for speculation by the girls confined at Dixon. They wondered if he were really deaf and dumb or just faking. The fact that he was accused of killing a woman may or may not have been known to them. It is highly possible that someone may have heard about it from one of the aides and passed the knowledge along. It is known that the older girls talked about Donald a good deal, mainly about his annoying sexual advances, and many of them had reason to resent him.

In late August, it was decided to allow a few girls into the all-male setting of Donald's shop group. One of these girls spotted Donald and, without any provocation, made an insulting gesture with her finger. Donald lost his head and went for her, squealing with rage. The girl ran in terror and only quick intervention on the part of the shop foreman saved her from harm. The incident was a shock to Merlyn Niedens, director of the I.T.U. unit, and he immediately dashed off a memo to Dr. Rybak.

'... I'm not so certain we should recommend that Donald Lang poses no threat to the community and that his charges be dropped. An incident occurred on A-14 that has somewhat shaken my conviction. We have observed Donald primarily in a male setting and his interaction with females has been limited. Recently, we have included females into our workshop. On Wednesday, one of these girls insulted Donald with a vulgar gesture. He became highly disturbed and took off in pursuit of her. Fortunately this was a supervised setting. True, Donald was provoked, but he was not operating in any unusual situation or stress. I have never observed this degree of hostility towards a male resident. Possibly he is harbouring a great deal of anger towards members of the opposite sex and this was unleashed by this provocation. The alleged incident that confined Donald involved a female. I was preparing a letter for Mr. Goldberg concerning Donald's case, but I would like your opinion in regard to this incident before any recommendations are made.'

The idea of fully endorsing Donald was abandoned. Instead, a letter was sent to Goldberg which, if anything, would strengthen the Circuit Court's position that Donald was unfit to stand trial. The letter was dated 10 Sepember 1969.

Jerome Goldberg
Special Counsel
Department of Mental Health
1500 State of Illinois Building
Chicago, Illinois

Re: Donald Lang
Competency to stand trial

Dear Mr. Goldberg:
At the present time, Donald Lang is unable to carry on any

meaningful conversation either verbally or by any type of manual alphabet. The only way Donald is able to communicate is with direct, simple gestures.

Donald is unable to comprehend the reason for his placement at Dixon State School. When shown photographs relating to the incident that resulted in his commitment to the Department of Mental Health, he is unable to relate this to the present placement.

Donald is well oriented in a known situation. When he is performing in such a setting, he is able to function appropriately.

On the basis of the above, it is doubtful whether Donald could co-operate in any meaningful fashion in a trial.

Very truly yours,
David Edelson
Superintendent, Dixon State School

Lowell Myers had not been relying on letters of recommendation to help his case. What people thought of Donald would not be taken into consideration by the Supreme Court. That learned body dealt only in hard legal facts. Myers had submitted his brief to the Supreme Court with that in mind. He divided his argument into six main sections and provided ample, and he hoped conclusive, legal evidence to substantiate each point. They were ...

I

A deaf-mute cannot be imprisoned for life because he has the handicap of being unable to communicate.

Robinson v. California 370 U.S. 660, 8 L. Ed. 2d 758,82 S. Ct. 1417 (1962)

II

A deaf-mute cannot be imprisoned for life because he is merely accused of a criminal offence (without ever being given a trial, and without ever being convicted).

(Eight cases were referred to as precedents for this point, as well as four amendments to the United States Constitution.)

III

A deaf-mute who cannot communicate has a right to lead a

normal life. He has a right to marry, a right to travel and a right to work. These rights cannot be arbitrarily taken away from him.

(Three test cases followed for reference.)

IV

It was never intended that the Illinois Statute, (Chapter 38, Section 104 of the Illinois Revised Statutes) would be applied to a person such as Donald Lang.

V

A Statute can be constitutional in one application and entirely unconstitutional in another application.

> *Sniadach v. Family Finance Corp.*, 395 U.S. 337 23
> L. Ed. 2d 349, 89 S. Ct. (1969)

and Myers' big gun ...

VI

A deaf-mute who cannot communicate and who is accused of a crime has a fundamental legal right to a criminal trial (so that he can prove he is innocent). He cannot be imprisoned indefinitely, without such a trial.

> *Regina v. Roberts* (1953) All England Reports 340

This was the body of the brief, with each argument resting squarely on solid legal ground. Myers' conclusion offered the Court two alternatives:

1. The defendant is given a criminal trial (even though he cannot communicate) so that he will have an opportunity to prove that he is innocent. Although he is handicapped, he should be given the best opportunity possible under the circumstances to prove that he is innocent.
2. The other alternative is that the defendant is given no criminal trial at all, and he is left in the custody of the Department of Mental Health forever. In this event, the defendant never gets any opportunity at all to prove he is innocent; and yet he is still imprisoned for life. This is unconstitutional.

   The judgment issued by the trial court (which denied him a Writ of habeas corpus should be reversed.

The Illinois Supreme Court accepted the brief in May 1970—
Docket No. 42777—Agenda 68. The fate of Donald Lang,
although not exactly in the lap of the Gods, was in very strong
hands indeed.

For every argument there is a rebuttal. The State of Illinois,
acting through Assistant Attorney General James B. Zagel,
prepared its brief on behalf of the Department of Mental
Health. It was much shorter than the one Myers had submitted
—a nine-page hammer blow aimed at the question of Donald
Lang's competency, or lack of it. They ignored *Regina v. Roberts*
and most of the other five points that Myers had stressed. Their
point was simple—Donald was incompetent, and until he was
proved competent there could be no discussion, let alone a
reversal of the lower court's opinion. The Argument stated, in
part :

> ... Donald Lang, the relator, is a deaf-mute and an illiterate.
> He presently knows no sign language or method of silent
> communication ... the relator stands as an adjudicated in-
> competent. He cannot be tried for murder without violating
> his constitutional rights ... It is apparent that the People
> are powerless to act until relator has been restored (to com-
> petency).
> The relator sought release by Writ of habeas corpus ...
> The State has not failed in its duty to treat the relator. The
> relator has refused treatment and has not learned to com-
> municate. However, this is not the responsibility of the State.
> The relator's complaint is not one of changed conditions ren-
> dering a lawful incarceration unlawful—the relator bases his
> claim on the lack of change. If anything, by relator's premi-
> ses, the conditions existing at the time of the lawful commit-
> ment, still exist and still justify the commitment.
> It must also be noted that the relator's position contains
> certain inherent contradictions. His attorney has filed a peti-
> tion verified by himself stating that 'Donald Lang wishes to
> be placed on trial ...' Further, counsel states that 'communi-
> cation with Donald Lang would not be needed at a trial.' The
> plain fact of the matter is that if Donald Lang cannot com-
> municate at all, it is impossible to see how counsel can
> state that his client 'wishes' a trial. On the face of this

record, it is not at all clear that the relator is hopelessly incompetent to stand trial. The conclusions of the Superintendent of the Dixon State School are ambiguous at best. His letter shows a refusal to co-operate in efforts to teach Lang to communicate. But a refusal to communicate or to learn how to communicate does not constitute incompetency per se. Inability to co-operate is incompetency. Refusal to co-operate is not. The Superintendent says that relator is functioning at a nearly normal level of performance in areas other than communication. This, if true, might support a finding of *refusal to communicate* rather than inability to communicate.

And again, we reiterate that counsel asserts that his client 'wishes' a trial and that he 'merely happened to be there when the crime took place'. All of this language implies that there is some level of communication attained by relator and that there exists a present ability to communicate or to learn to communicate. Perhaps this evidence is sufficient to justify a finding of competency. The proper procedure for determining this issue is not habeas corpus but is, instead, a recovery hearing ...

The State was asking the Supreme Court to place Donald Lang back on the merry-go-round of a competency hearing. They would have Dr. Myklebust, or men of his stature, waiting in the wings with maze tests and block puzzles. The result of such a hearing would be a foregone conclusion.

Lowell Myers, as Relator-Appellant (on behalf of Donald Lang), was allowed the final word. He attacked the State's contention that Donald Lang's attorney should petition for a new competency hearing under Section 104 of the Illinois Revised Statutes.

... The person who wrote the statute assumed that anyone who could not 'understand' a trial would be severely mentally ill and therefore should be committed to a mental institution. That was a natural assumption, but he forgot about deaf-mute people like Donald Lang who might not be able to 'understand' a trial, and yet still might be perfectly normal, apart from their handicap ...

The attorney for the State argues in his Brief that I should have filed a Petition saying that Donald has now recovered, and that he is now 'competent' under this statute.

I did not file such a Petition because it would not have been true ... Donald is just as 'incompetent' today *under this statutory definition*—as he was two years ago. Donald has not changed; and the statutory definition has not changed ...

The attorney for the State argues that if Donald cannot communicate, then Donald could not have given his lawyer any instructions about the handling of this case ... In other words, the attorney for the State implies that if Donald cannot communicate then Donald's lawyer is not permitted to take any effective action on his behalf; due to lack of instructions.

This argument is totally incorrect. This is like saying that if a lawyer is appointed to be guardian for a minor child, the lawyer cannot do anything—because the child did not instruct the lawyer to do that ...

In exactly the same way, Donald's lawyer has the duty to take all legal steps necessary to get Donald out of his present life imprisonment. The lawyer must act for Donald because Donald cannot act for himself.

Because Donald is handicapped does not mean that the lawyer is also handicapped.

... The State points out that Donald seems to have communicated with his lawyer to some extent ... The attorney for the State seems puzzled ... as to whether or not Donald can communicate. The answer is that communication is always a matter of *degree*, and that there are many *types* of communication. For example, anyone who has seen one of the old-time silent movies with Charlie Chaplin will testify that Charlie Chaplin was able to communicate very well with his audiences. He could make the audience laugh. He could make them cry. He could communicate very complicated situations and conflicting emotions—and he could do all of this *without using a single word* ...

For ordinary everyday activities, language is not really needed. It's nice to have, but it's quite possible to get along without it ... Suppose that you were suddenly transported to a city in Russia. You would not understand what the people were talking about, and you would not be able to read the street signs or the newspapers. Yet, you would still be an intelligent person and you could probably get along quite well. (Most tourists do.) Gestures and pantomime would be quite sufficient for everyday purposes.

But, suppose that while you are in this Russian city the

police suddenly put handcuffs on you and take you to a courtroom where everybody is speaking Russian, and you cannot understand a word of it. This is essentially the situation that Donald Lang now occupies.

If a person has a serious case of aphasia he will never learn any language of any kind. It makes no difference how many times a symbol or a word is repeated to him. If the necessary part of the brain is damaged, he simply will not learn. The individual *himself* very quickly realizes this. He gives up the attempt, and turns to other activities ...

Donald probably resists going to class because he already knows from experience that the attempt to learn a language is hopeless. Donald had probably known that since he was five or six years old.

Suppose that a man tries to teach a cow to eat sawdust. The cow will not 'learn' to do that. (It's impossible for the cow.) Moreover, the cow will soon start to 'resist' being taught. The instructor will write in his report—'This cow is not co-operating!' That would be perfectly true, but the simple reason would be that the cow cannot learn and that is why the cow is resisting. If we took a man who had ... shaking palsy and tried to 'teach' him to walk a tightrope, it would be an impossible task and the man would very soon start to 'resist' such instruction.

We must keep in mind that Donald communicates by means of pantomime and actions. When he 'refuses' to co-operate with the instructor, that refusal is a direct form of communication ... Donald is 'telling' the instructor: 'I cannot learn this. You are wasting your time.' ...

... To summarize the entire matter, the State is entitled to delay the criminal trial in order to make a bona fide effort to educate the defendant and teach him to communicate. However, if the attempt fails, then the criminal trial must not be delayed any longer. At that time, the defendant becomes entitled to have his day in court ... Donald's trial cannot be delayed any further. He has a constitutional right to prove that he is innocent of the criminal charge against him.

Respectfully submitted
Lowell J. Myers

There was nothing to do now but wait. At the State capital

in Springfield, the seven justices of the Supreme Court would take their time. Docket number 42777 was not a matter to be judged lightly—or in haste.

Spring finally came to the Dixon School after a long, hard winter. Keeping four thousand young residents occupied during the cold winter months taxed the aides and counsellors to the limit of their ingenuity. A complex of ultramodern playgrounds had been constructed the previous October, but there had been few days mild enough for their use. Now, the Sears and Stuart List experimental playgrounds with their vast arrays of swings, slides, geodesic climbers and modular play structures were crowded with children. The older boys ran and shouted on the basketball courts, shirts off, relishing the sun.

Donald Lang was not among them. He sat on his bunk in Cottage A-14, drowsy from the effects of 100mg of Sparine that had been injected into him. The tranquillizer had been prescribed by Dr. Rybak so that Donald would remain calm and sleepy during the long drive ahead of him. The Intensive Therapy Unit at Dixon had been closed and the inmates of Cottage A-14 were being readied for transfer to the Lincoln State School near Peoria.

The Lincoln School was similar to Dixon—pleasant surroundings and fine old buildings. There was no provision for security at the school and it was thought that Donald might be less of a problem if he were kept isolated from the rest of the inmates. Instead of assigning him to one of the crowded dormitories, Donald was placed in the custody of John Loeffler, the school's maintenance man. It was a wise move. Loeffler could relate to the silent, young, black man and seemed to understand his needs. He put him to work, mainly at gardening, and showed him how to operate the power lawn mower—a tractor-like machine that towed a string of grass cutters behind it. The machine was similar in operation to the forklift jeep that Donald had driven during his years at the market. He was good at his job—and happy.

Many crops of tall summer grass had fallen beneath the cutter blades when, on 29 September 1970, the Supreme Court handed down its decision.

'The appellant, Donald Lang, an illiterate deaf-mute, herein

113

referred to as defendant ...' So began the opinion as delivered by Justice Marvin F. Burt. Justice Burt synopsized the case against Donald, from the murder indictment on 9 December 1965, to the present time ...

The State contends that the proper remedy for the defendant is to seek restoration to competency under the provisions of the Code of Criminal Procedure ... section 104-3(b). To this the attorney for the petitioner replies that he could not file a petition for recovery honestly because he could not state that there had been any change of status of the petitioner's incompetence.

... A special programme was set up to teach him sign language ... but apparently the defendant is not learning and the department believes that is because he does not wish to learn. There is no allegation or intimation that this defendant is in fact 'insane' so that any criminal proceeding against him would be void ...

... The petitioner argues that in this case Donald Lang may be incompetent because of a defect in his brain which would cause him to be technically mentally incompetent in the area of speech but nowhere else.

We agree that it is frequently difficult, if not impossible, to distinguish between physical and mental or psychological handicaps ...

Although the facts in this case are unique in American jurisprudence ... there is an English case, *Regina v. Roberts* ... in which the court dealt with a similar situation ...

This court is of the opinion that this defendant, handicapped as he is and facing an indefinite commitment because of the pending indictment against him, should be given an opportunity to obtain a trial to determine whether or not he is guilty as charged or should be released.

Therefore, the order of the circuit court is reversed and the cause remanded with directions to reinstate this case and proceed to trial of the pending indictment against this defendant Donald Lang; that Lowell J. Myers be continued as attorney for this defendant for trial; that the defendant be arraigned, and that the trial of this case be expedited in the circuit court.

After four years and nine months, Donald Lang and Lowell Myers would have their day in court.

CHAPTER IX

There was one delay. The State filed a petition for 'Clarification' with the Supreme Court, asking how such a trial could be, or should be, conducted. After all, they said, Donald Lang was a deaf-mute. What procedures should they follow in order to deal with such a handicap on the part of the defendant?

Lowell Myers replied ... 'I have written a book on the subject of deaf-mute cases and I will be happy to give a free copy to the State's attorneys ...'

The subject of 'Clarification' was resolved and on 3 December 1970, Lowell Myers was able to file his first motion for the defendant—a request to inspect the physical evidence in the case. Within a month Donald would be formally arraigned and a trial date set. Calendars were crowded, but it seemed likely that this case would be squeezed in ahead of others, as though to make up for the five-year delay. There was a lot for Myers to do. He wasn't coming into court with Donald to face Dr. Myklebust or Dr. Haines this time. The State wouldn't be trying to convince a jury that Donald Lang was an imbecile, but that he had wilfully murdered a woman in a dark alley— and Illinois had not abolished the death penalty.

To the Chicago Police Department, it was Case No. 65-8064-M, Williams, Ernestine—Homicide. The records were available upon request, all stamped with big, black letters ...

CLEARED

HOMICIDE 4

The records told the story of a crime, just one of thousands that Homicide 4 had dealt with over the years. The reports were poorly typed, tapped out with two fingers by overworked detectives.

... beat car 1207 assigned at 0735 hours. Upon arrival assignment was turned over to beat car 1281, Sergeant Curran, beat car 1271, Spieser and Kelly and beat 1207, Tucker. Victim was found lying on her right side at the bottom of a cement stairway behind a partially open door ...

... a pair of man's jockey shorts with blood on them was found in the gangway 10 feet north of where the body was found. The shorts, jockey, white, size 30 with a Hanes label, was inventoried under #552379 ...

VICTIM: WILLIAMS Ernestine, F/N, Age 38, 1622 W. Washburne, 1st floor.

INJURY: Stab wound centre of chest, contusions of left eye and mouth, contusions of neck.

TAKEN TO: Cook County hospital by patrol #1271.

PRONOUNCED: Pronounced D.O.A. by Dr. Z. Solbos at 0910 hrs. 12 November 65.

IDENTIFICATION: Made at scene by brother, CHATMAN, A. J., M/N, Age 43.

DATE AND TIME: Body found 0600 hrs., 12 Nov. 1965—occurred 0400 hrs., 12 Nov. 1965.

LOCATION: Outside rear stairway at 1654 W. Washburne.

MOTIVE: Probable rape or attempt rape.

WEAPON: Probable fists and unknown sharp object (not recovered).

WITNESSES: Found body—HARRIS Mamie, F/N, Age 32, 1652 W. Washburne, 2nd floor. BRADLEY George, M/N, Age 57, 1652 W. Washburne, 1st floor, rear. Heard conversation and arguing between 0300 and 0400 hours.

WITNESSES: ANDERSON, Pauline, 1652 W. Washburne. Stated she heard a woman scream and some conversation in the gangway at about 0400 hrs. but states she was afraid to get involved and did not look out.

A canvass was made of the area and all persons found were questioned but none were able to add anything to the investigation. Some stated there were teenage boys waiting around the block to prey on drunks coming home but none were able to give any specific information.

There has been no inquest set at this writing.

Investigation being carried out by 2nd watch personnel with results to be reported.

REPORT OF: Det. W. Brodersen #3804, Det. W. Boyd #3439.

CLEARED
HOMICIDE 4

IN CUSTODY: LANG, Donald S. M/N 19 yrs. of age. 1440 W. 14th St. Apt. 105. Employed as a day labourer by Harper Motor lines. (Subject is a deaf-mute).

INVESTIGATION: In continuing the investigation into subject Homicide Det. Louis Denson, Star #2371 assigned to Homicide/Sex Unit, DDA #4 contacted one JACKSON, Lee M/N 61 yrs. of age. Jackson told Det. Denson that he had been in the tavern at the south-east corner of Paulina St. and Roosevelt Rd. on the evening of 11 November 1965. He further stated that he had observed the victim in the tavern drinking and playing records until at approximately 2200 hours when she left with what Jackson described as 'A short coloured man who is deaf and dumb.'

Myers had read these reports before, as well as the transcript from the coroner's inquest held on 13 November 1965. Now he read them again, over and over. They constituted the bare facts of a slum killing. A prostitute danced in front of a juke-box and then walked off into the Chicago night at 2200 hours with 'a short coloured man who is deaf and dumb'. She had shouted at old Mr. Jackson that she would buy him a beer when she got back. She had asked her friend, Mary Jane Carter, a Female/Negro, aged 46 years, to hold her red coat until she returned. She never did return. She died in a trash-clogged alley with her red ski pants down below her knees and her red sweater wadded behind her back.

Twenty-two hundred hours—ten p.m. The short, deaf and dumb coloured man, later identified as Donald Lang, returned to the tavern at approximately twelve-thirty a.m., approached Mary Jane Carter, pointed at the coat she was holding and then gestured in the direction of the alley, where the victim was found at six o'clock that morning.

Why, Myers asked himself, had Donald returned to the tavern? Had Ernestine indicated to Donald that she was cold and wanted to have her coat? Myers tried to picture the scene in his mind and form some kind of logical scenario of that night's confusing events.

First ... they had left the tavern at 10 p.m. after buying a bottle of wine. Donald had held up some money; so, in the light of Ernestine's profession, his desires were clear. He wanted sex and was willing to pay for it. Ernestine wanted a party. She was a prostitute, not a back-alley wino. Her clothing was good. It seemed illogical to Myers that she had been planning to drink the wine and have sex with Donald in the cold night air when her apartment was only a short walk away.

Dorothy Hunter had seen them walking, as she so testified at the coroner's inquest ...

Q. You are the one that was walking down the street?

A. Yes.

Q. And saw Ernestine Williams and Lang walking down the street?

A. Yes.

Q. And you turned around and they were gone?

A. Yes.

Q. And the closest thing to you was the alley?

A. Yes.

The Deputy Coroner had mentioned 'and you turned around and they were gone' and 'the closest thing to you was the alley'. Dorothy Hunter had never said such things when she had first been interrogated. Detective James Anderson had taken a statement from her on 12 November 1965, at 8.00 p.m.—fourteen hours after the body had been discovered, five hours after Donald's arrest.

Q. During the time you were in the tavern did you see Donald Lang?

A. Yes, I saw him, but I only know him to be called the deaf and dumb boy.

Q. Did you see him and Ernestine together at any time while you were in the tavern?

A. Not in the tavern. Outside the tavern ... I had gone home to turn off the gas under my cooking. When I was walking back to the tavern and as I turned the corner of Paulina and Washburne, I saw the two of them come out of the tavern door. As I was walking on Paulina on the east side of the street, I passed right by them as they were going south on Paulina Street. As I got right next to them, Ernestine waved her hand

and said, 'I'll be right back.' I went into the tavern and stayed there until midnight or 12.30 a.m. Neither of them had come back up to the time I left.

Q. Is there anything further you wish to add to this statement?

A. No. That is all.

A minor discrepancy to be sure, but Dorothy Hunter's testimony in front of the coroner had planted in the jury's mind a vision of Donald Lang and Ernestine ducking up the alley. They may have done so, then again they may have kept on walking south on Paulina Street to Washburne. Ernestine lived on Washburne. It seemed reasonable to assume that she had taken him to her place. Testimony of patrons of the tavern had shown Ernestine to have been in high spirits that fatal night. She had been drinking, dancing, looking for fun. Ernestine was thirty-eight years old, Donald was twenty.

He may have been a deaf-mute, but he was strong and virile. His sexual prowess may have led her to change her mind about going back to the tavern to buy a sixty-one-year-old man a beer. After two hours with Donald, she could have decided to settle for one trick that night. Could she have told him to go to the tavern and get her coat? Perhaps. Donald could be 'told' to do many things through gestures and pantomime. He had seen her leave her coat with Mary Jane Carter. Ernestine could have made her wants known. Donald did go to the tavern and he did approach Mary Jane and 'ask' for the coat. He did gesture towards the alley—or did he? He had simply made a gesture. He could have been pointing in the direction of Ernestine's house.

Rebuffed by Mary Jane Carter, Donald could then have gone back to Ernestine Williams and stayed with her until the small hours of the morning. They could have left her apartment together—Donald to go home, Ernestine to get something to eat, or to meet the man who was her pimp. (This man was never mentioned at the coroner's inquest or in any of the police reports, but Donald's older brother had seen him hanging around his property. Everyone in the neighbourhood knew Ernestine.) Their route could have taken them through the gangway next to 1654 Washburne, a three-foot-wide passage that connected Washburne Street with the alley that ran into Roosevelt Road. Someone could have been laying in wait in the shadows. There was 'conversation' and 'argument'—according to George Bradley and Pauline Anderson. The words had been loud enough to wake them. If Donald had been alone with Ernestine in that dark place, it would have been a very one-sided exchange. The 'conversation' and 'argument' were followed by a scream. Both witnesses agreed that the time had been between three and four a.m.—nearly six hours after Donald and Ernestine had left the tavern with their bottle of wine.

Death had followed argument. There had been blows, hard punches to Ernestine's head, then a knife thrust to her chest. There had been a great deal of blood. Some of that blood was on the clothing that the police had taken from Donald's home, but Myers had no way of knowing how much blood until the court complied with his petition to inspect the physical evidence. Blood on his clothing did not prove that Donald had killed Ernestine. According to the police report ... 'Victim was battered about the head and suffered excessive bleeding from the mouth ...' Anyone who has sat at the ringside during a particularly vicious prize-fight knows that blood can fly a long way. Donald could have been very close to Ernestine when she was attacked. He had seen the attack ... seen the beating and the stabbing. His actions after being arrested were construed as a confession. They could just as easily have been taken as the testimony of a witness. There had been his actions in the police station when he had plucked a ballpoint pen from a detective's shirt pocket and made a stabbing motion with it. Then, later, when he was driven to the tavern ...

(Sergeant Denson speaking at the coroner's inquest) ...

'... Donald Lang stood outside the car and motioned to go. He left the tavern, walked to the alley, into the alley to this gangway, through the gangway to the doorway where the victim had been found.'

Q. When he arrived at that point, what did he do then?

A. He made a motion, I wasn't there, but from Detective Hurbing, he made a motion as if to struggle and at the same time a stabbing motion and that's about all I know about that.

It had been sufficient for the coroner's jury to recommend that Donald Lang be held on a charge of murder.

If not Donald Lang, then who? Lowell Myers could not afford the luxury of speculation. Speculation meant nothing in a murder trial. The State prosecutor would give the jury facts —and a solid chain of circumstantial evidence. Lowell Myers needed facts of his own, but where would he get them? Not from silent Donald Lang.

12 January 1971. Lowell Myers appeared in court for a ruling on his first petition in the case. The Honourable Earl E. Strayhorn, one of the few black judges of the Circuit Court, ordered the State to turn over to Myers a list of the evidence they had and ruled that Myers was entitled to inspect that evidence. State Prosecutor Nicholas Mothersway then handed Myers a four-page document. It was dated 2 December 1965, and catalogued all of the physical evidence in possession of the police department relative to the murder of Ernestine Williams ...

CASE NO. 65-8064-M

On 12 November 1965, Detective Anderson, of Area 4 Homicide/Sex, submitted the following items to the laboratory requesting examination:

1. One pair of men's trousers, hereinafter referred to as exhibit K-1.
2. One jacket, hereinafter referred to as exhibit K-2.

Exhibit K-1 is a pair of light green 'Levi' trousers. Bloodstains are present on the front and rear panels. Extracts of these stains have been made and are retained in the laboratory file.

Exhibit K-2 is a man's leather, zippered front, waist-length jacket, beige in colour. The upper right and left shoulder areas of both sleeves are torn. Several bloodstains are present on the exhibit.

On 12 November 1965, Technicians Bell and Bolt of the Crime Laboratory, Mobile Unit, submitted the following item to the laboratory for examination.

1. One pair of men's shorts, hereinafter referred to as exhibit Q-1.

Exhibit Q-1 is a pair of men's shorts bearing a 'Hanes— size 30' label. Bloodstains are present on the upper front and crotch areas. Dirt and debris are adhering to the exhibit.

On 12 November, Detective Anderson submitted the following item to the laboratory for examination.

1. One knife, hereinafter referred to as exhibit Q-2, and

identified as having been recovered from a wastebasket in room 205, located at 943 West Maxwell Street (Police Headquarters).

Exhibit Q-2 is a pearl-handled, three-bladed pocket knife ... one side of the pearl handle is missing. Preliminary chemical tests for blood yielded negative reactions.

Extracts of reddish-brown stains present on exhibit K-1 were subjected to various chemical and serological tests. The results are as follows: The stains are human bloodstains of group 'AB'.

There then followed a list of the clothing taken from Ernestine Williams and the result of a laboratory analysis of Ernestine's blood. It was type 'AB'.

The State's case was wholly circumstantial in nature, but a man doesn't have to be found with a weapon in his hand and a corpse at his feet to be hung for murder. The words ... 'a reasonable doubt' are part of every judge's instructions to a jury in murder trials. Those words would hang heavily over the head of Donald Lang. The State could prove without any doubt that Donald had left the tavern with Ernestine Williams. They could prove that her blood—or blood of the same type—was on his clothes, and that he had led police officers to the scene of the crime without any prompting. Lowell Myers did not doubt the fact that Donald had been with Ernestine when she was killed; he just did not believe that Donald had done the killing.

The State had a bloody pair of pants, a torn and bloody jacket, a bloody pair of undershorts and a knife. All Myers had was his conviction.

Blood on the pants—on the front and on the back? Why on the back? And what did the stains look like? Were they great saturated splotches, or scattered dots? The report did not state. It was important to find out. If the blood on the back of the pants were droplets it could mean that Donald had thrown himself to the ground when the attack occurred, that he was lying face down in the alleyway and was sprayed with Ernestine's blood as she was hit and hit again.

It was just speculation and Myers knew it, but the evidence

might lend substance to his theory. Somehow, he felt certain that it would.

The crime laboratory of the Chicago Police Department is located on the fifth floor of a South State Street building. Lowell Myers met Nicholas Mothersway there on a cold January afternoon to examine the evidence against Donald Lang. The court order authorizing this examination by Myers was handed to the man in charge of the laboratory and the articles of evidence were removed from the files and placed on a table. Myers stared down at a small collection of glassine envelopes with identification tags stapled to the edges. Donald Lang's pants had been reduced to two scraps of cloth no more than two inches square and four scraps about the size of a dime. The jacket was one two-inch square of beige cloth. The underwear, 'Hanes—size 30', was nothing but an inch of ragged lint. There was no knife.

Myers was outraged. Where, he wanted to know, were the rest of the garments?

'Disposed of,' the laboratory man said.

'And the knife?'

'Disposed of.'

'All right,' Myers said. 'Then how about photographs of the pants, jacket, underpants and knife. You do have photographs, don't you?'

There was only one photograph—of the underpants—but the jockey shorts had been folded in such a manner that only about one quarter of their outside surface could be seen, and none of the inside surface.

Myers looked again at what was left of Donald's pants and jacket. The rust-coloured stain on the tiny bits of cloth were large enough for serological testing, but no conclusions could be reached when these were looked at with the naked eye. There was no way that Myers could give credence to his theory of *sprayed* blood on the back of the pants. No way at all.

Myers returned to his office and began work on a flurry of motions for presentation to the court. He had his secretary phone Genettia Lang Ellis, Donald's sister, to ask her to come to the office at once. Myers was opening a two-pronged attack on the State's evidence in the case. His first motion was for the court to strike the indictment against his client due to *Intentional Destruction of Evidence by the State*. He wrote:

'... In regard to the jacket and pants, the State, through its agents, has deliberately destroyed over ninety-nine per cent of the items. It has retained less than one per cent of the items. The State believes that the one per cent that they have retained is favourable to the State, and at the trial of this case, they will seek to put the one per cent of the items before the jury—even though the State has deliberately destroyed the other ninety-nine per cent of the exhibits, without *permission* from the Court.

I believe that the missing ninety-nine per cent of the exhibits contained important evidence in favour of the defendant. Since the State has deliberately destroyed this evidence, I will be unable to use it before the jury.

In regard to the underpants, I believe that a comparison of the blood marks on the underwear as compared to the blood marks on the pants would have proven that they were worn by two different persons at two different times, and that the blood patterns did not match *at all*. Since the State has destroyed ninety-nine per cent of both the pants and the underpants, this evidence in favour of the defendant has been totally lost—forever.

In regard to the knife, I believe that tracing the ownership of the knife would have shown that it did not belong to the defendant but belonged to a different person entirely. Since the knife has been totally destroyed by the State and no pictures of the knife were taken before it was intentionally destroyed by the State, this evidence in favour of the defendant no longer exists.

In this Motion, we are concerned with the question of whether the State can pick out one per cent of an item, which the State feels is favourable to it, and then destroy the remaining ninety-nine per cent of the item so that the defendant will lose that part of the exhibit which was in *his* favour.

The action of the State's agents in this case has done the defendant an irreparable injury. This deliberate destruction of vital evidence has perhaps made it impossible for the defendant to establish his innocence.

The above actions by the State's agents were a direct

violation of the defendant's legal rights and constitutional rights ...

As to whether the actions by the State's agents will make them subject to a criminal prosecution for the destruction of evidence, I express no opinion.

As to whether the Prosecutor had any part in this destruction of evidence, I express no opinion.

I move on behalf of the defendant for an order striking the Indictment, and ordering the defendant to be released. And for an order that upon the trial of this case, the State may not use *any part* of the four items of evidence mentioned above; that the State may not mention or refer to the four items of evidence in any manner, and that the entire amount of each of these items be suppressed as evidence ...'

There is no defence quite as good as a strong offence. Myers was determined to hit the prosecution where it hurt, to force them to come into court without any physical evidence at all. When Genettia arrived, Myers took the following affidavit:

'My name is Genettia Lang Ellis. I am the sister of Donald Lang, the defendant in this case.

On or about 13 November 1965, two police officers came to the apartment where I was then living. They knocked on the door of the apartment and showed me their police badges and told me that they were policemen. They asked me if they could come in and I told them that they could ... At the time that the policemen entered the apartment, I was seventeen years old and a minor ... The policemen asked me for Donald's clothes and I went into a different room and got his pants and jacket and I gave them to the policemen. They took the clothes and left with them.

The policemen did not show me any kind of a warrant.

The policemen did not tell me that I had a legal right to refuse to let them enter; or to refuse to give them the clothes. I did not know I had those legal rights ... I TAKE OATH THIS STATEMENT IS TRUE.'

Myers attached the affidavit to a motion in which he claimed that the search and seizure had been a violation not only of Illinois law, but a violation of the 4th and 14th Amendments

125

of the United States Constitution. He requested that the court order the suppression of this evidence and forbid the State prosecutors from making any reference to it during the trial.

A copy of these motions, and the affidavit, were received by the State's Attorney's office on 21 January, less than three weeks before the case was to come to trial. Without the use of that evidence the State was left with one argument—that Donald Lang had walked out of the Romeo tavern with Ernestine Williams on the night of 11 November 1965 and that, subsequently, Ernestine Williams had been beaten and knifed to death in an alley.

But the State was on shaky ground. It must rely heavily on its witnesses, making the connection between Lang and the dead woman. And the years in the ghetto had been as hard on them as they had been on Donald in prison. Lee Jackson, who had watched Ernestine and Donald leave the tavern, was dead. George Bradley, who had heard sounds of conflict in the alleyway, was dead. Pauline Anderson, who had also heard sounds of argument and struggle in the alley, could not be located. Mary Jane Carter, who had held Ernestine's coat, was dying in the municipal tuberculosis sanatorium. The State's case against Donald Lang was a castle built on sand.

Joseph Witkowski was considered one of the best prosecutors in the State's Attorney's office. He was wiry and intense, something of a nail biter, but all agreed that he was a sharp young lawyer and a born prosecutor. He went through all the papers relative to the upcoming case and his recommendation was terse—'Drop it.'

2 February 1971, a cold, black day. Lowell Myers arrived in Room 706 of the Criminal Courts Building, Judge Strayhorn's courtroom. The jury box was empty. This was a hearing, not a trial. Joseph Witkowski was present on behalf of the people of the State of Illinois, and Donald Lang was there, brought up from the county jail by a sheriff.

'Good morning,' Myers said. Rain slapped against the courtroom windows. It was not a good morning by any stretch of the imagination—except, perhaps, for Donald Lang and Lowell Myers. And what an incredibly long struggle it had been to reach this good morning of Donald Lang's day in court.

Witkowski acknowledged the greeting and then faced Judge Strayhorn and the court reporter.

'Let the record show that my name is Joseph Witkowski.

I am the assistant State's Attorney assigned to the case of the People versus Donald Lang.

'As the court is probably very well informed, Donald Lang is both deaf and dumb, and he has no ability to communicate. He is charged with murder under indictment number 65-3421. Your Honour, as a result of extensive background information we received on Donald Lang, and as a result of diligent investigative work by the State's Attorney's police, we have learned that three witnesses are not available to testify in the trial. We have our case based on a chain of circumstantial evidence. Each one of our witnesses would be necessary to prove our case. In this case we have three witnesses that would break the chain, and the State cannot prove its case.

'As a result of this, Your Honour, the State would move to *nolle prosse* the case against Donald Lang. I talked to Mr. Myers shortly before court and informed him that we would be willing to co-operate in any way we can with any State institution, either out-patient treatment, or whatever it might be, to help Donald Lang function better in today's society because of his communication problem.'

'Mr. Myers,' Judge Strayhorn said, 'the motion of the State is that this matter be *nolle prossed*. Do you have any statement to make?'

'No objection, Your Honour.'

Judge Strayhorn glanced over at Donald Lang who was now, although he was not yet aware of it, a free man.

'The court's concern has been partially answered by Mr. Witkowski,' the judge said. 'He states that the People are willing to assist in whatever way they can in placing your client in some institution where he may receive some sort of treatment which will prepare him to function, such as it will be, in today's society. I would like to ask you, Mr. Myers, if you intend to make some efforts to follow through in this connection?'

Myers nodded. 'Your Honour, before the defendant was arrested he was living a perfectly normal life. He was supporting himself and he lived a normal life with his family. His family is on the way down now, and they will take him home. I do think he should be educated and taught to communicate, if for no other reason than to avoid this problem in the future. I believe the family will make some efforts along that line. I will talk with them when they come down.'

'Very well,' Judge Strayhorn said. 'The order of the court will be—this case will be dismissed on the State's motion.'

The case of the People of Illinois versus Donald Lang was now over. After more than five years, Indictment Number 65–3421 was quashed in five minutes.

There was one final motion. Lowell Myers, as a court-appointed counsel, submitted a request for one thousand dollars in attorney's fees. It worked out, give or take an eternity of frustration, to less than two dollars an hour for his services to Donald Lang and the law.

The request was granted.

CHAPTER X

Donald Lang was a twenty-six-year-old man who had last seen the streets of Chicago as a twenty-year-old youth. The streets had not changed. Perhaps they were more crowded, and more dangerous than they had been in 1965, but the ABLA Housing Project was still on 14th Street and the South Water Market was still lined with produce trucks waiting to be unloaded. This had been Donald's world, the narrow circle of his horizon, and it was only natural for him to head back there.

Donald went first to live with his father and stepmother, Mary Lang, in their apartment on South State Street at 29th Street, but there was nothing in that section of the city that held any memories for him. He drifted back to the market. Mario Pullano was still there, a bit fatter than he had been nearly six years before, but time had not changed him much. He was now loading boss for one of the largest produce companies in the market and he accepted Donald's return without reservation.

There had been no serious effort to place Donald in an institution or school. He had been taken to the Jewish Vocational Workshop on South Franklin Street in the Loop by his brother, but he didn't stick around very long.

'He'd changed a lot since I'd seen him last.'

Katie Brown remembered Donald Lang. She, too, was deaf—and black. She remembered Donald when he had lived on the South Side. His mother used to bring him to the Ephatha Evangelical Lutheran Church for the Deaf on King Drive. A quiet boy ... shy ... so anxious to learn.

'It seemed that he wanted to learn so badly, but he was changeable. They'd give the service in sign language and after a while he'd get bored and restless. We'd play little games together. I'd hold his hand and then he'd squeeze mine hard and I'd take it away, very suddenly, and wouldn't let him hold it any more. I remember once he came up to a woman he'd never seen before and took both of her hands, and when she drew them away he grabbed them and hit her over the head—with her own hands. I guess he thought that was funny, but the woman was afraid.'

Katie Brown remembered.

'He was a lonely boy. He used to sit in his room a lot and—yes—eat watermelon and spit the seeds very carefully into his hand so they wouldn't get on the floor. I knew that he wanted to talk. He'd move his mouth and pretend he was speaking. He really felt that he *was* talking, and that was why it was so hard to teach him. I tried to show him that I was deaf, too, and make him read my lips, but it didn't work.'

Katie Brown had been more fortunate than Donald Lang. She had learned to read lips, and she had learned the sign language. She had gone to school—to grade school and high school and college. She was, in that early spring of 1971 when she saw Donald again after so many years, a graduate sociologist working with the deaf people at the Jewish centre.

'He lasted a week,' Katie Brown said. 'He was living with his stepmother and his father then, and he'd get the bus by himself and come on in. But he'd changed a lot since I'd seen him last in church. All those years—and that school. He wouldn't look at me, just turned away ... and then one day he didn't come in any more.'

Mrs. Dolly Gill had moved from the ABLA Housing Project and lived at 1526 Washburne when Donald was arrested. Ironically, this was only a few doors from where Ernestine Williams had been murdered. Mrs. Dolly Gill, mother of five children, remembered how Donald had saved the life of her boy Kenneth. She remembered how 'Donny' used to ring her bell and then hide. But that had been a long time ago.

'Donny always used to kiss me on the jaw when he came over, even when he got big. He was like a little kid that wanted to be patted and hugged. When he got back from prison he was so different. He didn't kiss me no more.'

Donald was drawn back to the area of the housing project and the market. This was his old turf and he began to spend more and more time at his brother's house on West Washburne, although he did not actually live there. He started work

130

at the market and Mario Pullano was glad to have him back, despite objections from some quarters. A man called him from the local Teamsters' office ...

'Keep that guy off the street and away from there or we'll get in trouble.'

'Look,' Pullano told him, 'the kid's been working around here for years. *Now* you think he's trouble!'

Donald stayed, unloading the big trucks and trailers, hustling for jobs just like the other workers. On the surface, nothing had changed, but there was an inner restlessness to Donald Lang. Sometimes he'd show up at the market every day without fail, and then he'd disappear for a week. No one knew where he went or what he was seeking.

Ghetto children measure their world in blocks. Five blocks away from *their* area is another country. Donald Lang had grown up with this philosophy. He had always stayed close to Washburne—Paulina—Roosevelt Road—and the ABLA Housing Project. The fifteen hundred block of West Madison Street is only fifteen city blocks north of this area, but it is a foreign land, isolated from Donald's section of the Near West Side by the broad concrete ribbon of the Eisenhower expressway. But there are attractions in the fifteen hundred block of West Madison Street—attractions that keep the cops from Maxwell Street Division, Area 4, very busy.

The Bull's Tavern is located at 1525 West Madison. It is an all black bar. Johnny Guitar's, just down the street, is a mixed black and white bar, while Huey's, next door to it, is all white. Black women hang out at The Bull's, waiting at the bar to sell their services, while the new ghetto children, the hillbilly girls from West Virginia and Kentucky, wait at Huey's. The white girls, most of them under age, float back and forth between Huey's and Johnny Guitar's, but they never show their faces at The Bull's. The black prostitutes consider The Bull's to be *their* turf.

There are hotels in the vicinity of The Bull's Tavern; the closest one being the Viceroy Hotel on Warren Boulevard, diagonally across the street. The Viceroy is well known to the Area 4 police as a hustle hotel, a place where rooms can be rented by the hour. The Viceroy is better than most; not all of its more than one hundred rooms are used for purposes of illicit sex. There are many permanent residents living in the hotel and the building is moderately clean and well cared for. Even the rooms that the prostitutes and their tricks utilize are tidied up after each visit; the sheets on the bed changed and clean towels placed in the bathroom.

In the late morning hours of Monday, the twenty-sixth of July 1971, a young woman by the name of Lillian Sheperd registered at the Viceroy Hotel with a man by the name of Russell Davis. Lillian Sheperd signed the register, the four dollars and seventy-five cents room rent was paid and the couple were handed a key by the desk clerk. They took the elevator to the second floor and walked down the hallway to Room 201.

The room was neat and clean. A window was open, the curtains stirring gently in the breeze. It was not an unpleasant room to be in on a muggy July morning—except for the smell.

Lillian Sheperd noticed the smell the moment she walked into the room. It was a sweetish, rancid odour, and she turned slowly in the middle of the room trying to locate its source. It seemed to her that it emanated from the closet. The door seemed to be stuck, but she gave it a good yank and it opened. Lillian Sheperd wished that it hadn't.

CASE REPORT/CHICAGO POLICE

Beat 1322 assigned by C.C.R. to see Mrs. McPhereon at the Viceroy Hotel lobby, 1519 W. Warren. On arrival R/Os were met by the janitor, Mr. Baul, who stated that there was a body in Room 201 closet ... R/O's notified the following ... A/4 Hom. Lt. Azzarello at 1211 hrs ...

Lieutenant Azzarello assigned two homicide detectives to investigate, and within minutes of the call being received, investigators James Padar and Philip Ducar were speeding to the scene. They arrived to find the hotel secured by officers from Beats 1322, 1384, 1390 and 1371. The coroner's office had been notified and the criminalistics division were on the way with the mobile unit. Bodies are found in the city of Chicago with depressing regularity, but the finding of one is not treated lightly.

INVESTIGATION: The reporting investigators received this assignment by radio at 1220 hours on 26 July 1971. Upon arrival at the crime scene it was noted that 013 District personnel had secured same and were awaiting the arrival of the crime lab and CID personnel. Room 201 is located at the east end of the north hallway on the second floor. The room is about 10' × 20' with a bathroom immediately to the right of the entrance. Access to the closet is blocked when the hall door is open. Upon entering the room, it was noted that the bed appeared freshly made and undisturbed. The room was generally neat and clean. A window at the far south end of the room was open and a strong odour was noted. Upon closing the hall door and opening the closet door, the body of the victim was observed lying face down, head to the north and feet to the south, with feet propped up along the south wall of the closet due to the restricted space. The body was clothed in a white girdle only ... said girdle being pulled up about the waist of the victim ...

Investigators Padar and Ducar were very thorough men. Padar, thirty-four and a bit on the plump side, had been with Homicide/4 for three years and had been attending night school for six years, working towards a degree in criminology and sociology. Philip Ducar was only twenty-six, new to homicide work but no less intense and conscientious than was his partner. Both men knew that they had a tough case on their hands.

'A mystery case,' Padar said. 'There are three kinds of homicides—"known but flown", which is just a tracking job—"smoking gun", where you've got the guy still standing over the body—and "mystery". Mystery is the toughest. There are four million people in the Chicago area.'

And one of them had killed the woman in Room 201 of the Viceroy Hotel.

INVESTIGATION: It should be noted that two pillows were

found lying on top of the body in the closet, and upon removal of the body, two blood-soaked sheets and the victim's clothing and purse were found on the closet floor. There was a great deal of blood ...

The bloody sheets drew attention to the immaculately-made bed. The two detectives stripped the bed of its clean sheets. The mattress beneath the sheets was unsullied. Padar flipped the mattress over and found 'a large stain of blood-like appearance near the head end of the bed, on both the mattress underside and the box spring top side.'

They left this for the crime lab men and went downstairs into the lobby to interrogate Lillian Sheperd, Russell Davis, the desk clerk and the janitor. No information that would be of any help in finding the killer, or in identifying the victim, was forthcoming from them. The investigators then talked to Mattie Ligon, the hotel manager. The finding of the bloody sheets and the pillows had cleared up a mystery for her. Mrs. Ligon stated that she had rented Room 201 to a Negro couple on the morning of 25th July at approximately 12.30 a.m. She believed that the man, who was young looking, signed the register card, but she wasn't positive about it. She had turned away for a moment when the card had been filled out, so it was possible that the woman had signed the card. That was the extent of Mattie Ligon's confusion. She was positive about everything else that took place during those early morning hours. The couple had walked up the main stairway to the second floor. Approximately two hours later, the man came down to the lobby by way of the side stairs. Mrs. Ligon was puzzled. She phoned Room 201 to find out the status of the woman. There was no answer, so she sent one of the maids to the room. The maid called down on the house phone and stated that the woman was not in the room and that the sheets and the pillows were missing from the bed. Mrs. Ligon thought that it was odd, but transient couples often did strange things at the Viceroy Hotel. She told the maid to remake the bed and get two new pillows from the linen closet.

Mrs. Ligon then told the officers that Rufus Knight, a long-time resident of the hotel, had been keeping her company in the lobby. Mr. Knight had been standing by the desk when the couple had entered. The young man had waved to Mr. Knight in a friendly manner and Mr. Knight had waved back. It was at this point, while the two men were making gestures at one another, that she realized the man was deaf and dumb.

James Padar was a painstaking man. He knew how to build a case one piece at a time so that there would be no gaps, no questions unanswered. He and Philip Ducar left the hotel and drove to the offices of the firm that owned the Viceroy Hotel. They wanted to check the room register cards that had been turned in early that Monday morning with the weekend cash receipts. They studied the cards that gave the history of Room 201 from the time of the victim's arrival to the discovery of the body. The victim and her friend had signed in as 'Mr. & Mrs. Joknos', no address. Room 201 had then been rented at 0445 hours on the morning of 25 July, and at 0915 hours. The room had then remained unoccupied until Lillian Sheperd and Russell Davis checked in. The time between the maid's report of missing sheets in Room 201 until the arrival of Lillian Sheperd was approximately thirty-two hours.

After looking over the registry cards, Padar checked in with other officers from Homicide 4 who were working on the case. One of the men he called was Detective Frank Bertucci.

Frank Bertucci had been a homicide detective for six years He was thirty-six years old, short, dark, stocky and tough. He had a good reputation among the Assistant State's Attorneys for turning in watertight evidence. Prosecutors never had to worry about cases falling apart in their hands when Frank Bertucci had done the investigative work. They kidded him a lot, calling him 'Columbo' because of his shaggy appearance and deceptively mild demeanour. His raincoat was missing its buttons, and ash from his cigar was always falling on to the front of his suit, but beneath this facade of bumbling gumshoe, he was sharp cop to the core.

Bertucci was at the Cook County morgue when he received the call from Detective Padar. He had examined the corpse of the 'Jane Doe' found at the Viceroy Hotel and was making arrangements for fingerprint identification. If the woman had been a prostitute, and his instinct for such matters led him to believe that she had been, there would probably be an arrest sheet on her and the prints would be on record. He felt certain that they would have the name of the victim within a few hours. The phone call from Padar was encouraging. Rufus Knight apparently had known the man who registered at the hotel with the victim. Mr. Knight, according to the hotel manager, worked at Wieboldt's department store on State Street. He had worked at the store for many years as a stock man and would be working there now. Bertucci left the morgue and drove to the Loop to interview the witness.

Rufus Knight was in his late forties, a mild-mannered, quiet man. He was very co-operative with Bertucci and told him everything that he wanted to know without hesitation. Yes, he had seen a man and a woman check into the hotel early Sunday morning. Yes, he had seen the woman many times but he didn't know her name. Yes, he knew the man; in fact, he had known him on and off for nearly fifteen years. His name was Lang, Donald Lang, but some people called him 'Dummy'.

By a strange coincidence, Bertucci had been talking about Donald Lang just a few days prior to this. Bertucci's wife had an uncle who worked at the South Water Market, and he had mentioned that 'Dummy Lang was back out and working at the market.' He had intimated to Bertucci that the truckers and warehousemen around the market thought that Lang had been persecuted by the police. 'He's a real nice guy,' the uncle had said, but Bertucci had his own opinion.

Five-oh-five p.m. Detectives Padar and Ducar returned to the Maxwell Street police station. It was a few minutes before a change of shift and Padar was debating whether or not to turn the case over to the third watch when Bertucci came in the door.

'You want Donald Lang,' Bertucci said. 'You'll find him working at the Strompolis Company, 117 South Water Market.'

The two young detectives were amazed. Neither one of them had ever heard of Donald Lang or knew anything about the earlier case. They thought Bertucci was clairvoyant, or a genius—or both.

Mario Pullano met them on the loading dock of the Strompolis Company, Quality Produce. Padar told him that they were looking for Donald Lang—and what they wanted him for. Pullano exploded.

'Jesus Christ! Every time you find a dead broad, you gonna blame it on the Dummy?'

The officers waited patiently until Mario Pullano had calmed down. He brought Donald to them and Ducar took out his handcuffs.

'Don't chain him!' Pullano yelled. 'He ain't an animal!'

Donald Lang was taken to the Maxwell Street station un-handcuffed. He kept staring at the two detectives but he was very co-operative, a model prisoner. He was also a unique one. The established police procedure for booking a suspect was pointless in Donald's case. Frank Bertucci went through the motions of reading Donald his rights. Donald just stared at him, uncomprehending. There was something about Donald's attitude that infuriated Bertucci. He felt, somehow, that Donald was trying to make a fool of him, that he was faking his disability. Bertucci had never read the results of any of the hearing tests that had been performed on Donald, but was acting on his own instincts and on the rumours he had heard from men who worked at the South Water Market. Donald's uncanny ability to function had led many people he worked with to believe he could hear. They were wrong. Bertucci was wrong.

'I think the son of a bitch can hear!' Bertucci said angrily. Bertucci is Italian. He made a gesture with his hand. He was standing behind Donald when he uttered the remark and made the gesture and Donald spun around, fists clenched in fury. It was an awkward moment for the arresting officers. Padar, after listening to what Mario Pullano had to say about Donald, was certain he was deaf and dumb. The incident did not shake that belief, but it puzzled him.

Again, Bertucci read Donald his rights, and again, Donald stared blankly at him. Bertucci then took out his pen and wrote several questions on a piece of paper in large, block letters ...

Do You Read and Write?
Do You Understand English?

Donald grabbed the pen from Bertucci's hand, picked up a blank piece of paper from a table and drew a picture with quick strokes of the pen. It was a curious drawing—crude, and yet somehow terribly expressive. He drew a jagged line in the shape of a stick, and a stick figure. After finishing the stick figure, he pointed to himself, indicating that he was that figure. At the opposite end of the first jagged line, he drew another stick figure with a curly mass of lines at the top to indicate hair. He made a gesture with his cupped hands to pantomime breasts. The drawing was clear to the policemen. A man and a woman—Donald Lang and 'Jane Doe'. Donald then drew a jagged, step-like line towards the top of the page, perpendicular to the first line. At the top of these 'stairs' he drew a big X. He paused for a moment, looked at the men around him, held up three fingers, pointed at the figure of the woman and then crossed the woman out with another large X.

It was an eerie experience. The officers stared at the drawing, not quite knowing what to make of it. They had the feeling that they were looking at the story of a crime, but how to interpret it? Was it a confession? What was the significance of the three fingers Donald had held up? There was no answer. The men placed their initials on the drawing and Padar took it preparatory to having it inventoried. As he started to leave the interrogation room, he noticed Donald's socks. They were thin white socks and there was a reddish-brown stain on one of them.

Padar motioned for the other men to come with him. When they stepped into the hall, he told them what he had seen. The stain had the appearance of dried blood. The officers then returned to the room. Donald was standing where they had left him, but he had rolled down his socks. The stain was no longer visible.

The long summer afternoon turned to dusk. Donald's family had been notified by Mario Pullano, and Donald's father appeared at the Maxwell Street station. He was asked by the police to return home and gather a change of clothing for his son, which he did.

Donald co-operated with the police in the removal of his clothes—except for his socks. It took some time, and a great many gestures on the part of the police, before Donald finally stripped off his socks and handed them to Detective Padar. The socks were placed in an envelope, inventoried, and sent to the crime lab for analysis.

The word that Donald Lang had been arrested spread quickly through the State's Attorney's office. On the basis of their previous experience with Donald, the men in that office were determined to make doubly sure that none of Donald's constitutional rights were in any way violated. Assistant State's Attorney Roland Banks arrived at Maxwell Street during the early part of the investigation and conferred with Bertucci and Padar. He also phoned Joseph Witkowski to keep him abreast of developments and to ask for guidance.

The police were moving swiftly. Bertucci, Padar and Ducar were sticking with the case, working overtime, determined to work all night if necessary. They wanted to wrap things up by acquiring enough evidence against Donald to have him booked for murder. The next step, after sending his clothing to the crime lab, was to establish without a shadow of doubt that he was the man who had checked into the hotel with the victim on the night of 24 July, and that he was the same man who had left the Viceroy Hotel alone during the early morning hours of 25 July. A patrol car was sent to the hotel to bring Rufus Knight and Mattie Ligon down to the station to be witnesses at a line-up.

Donald Lang is a deaf-mute man, Roland Banks warned the police. Do nothing that would make the line-up subject to controversy. Banks was like a man walking across thin ice, and his attitude was reflected in the way the police conducted the line-up at 8.45 that night. Donald was brought into the squad room along with five other young Negro males, none of whom were over the age of thirty. Absolute and complete silence was ordered from all concerned—the police as well as the persons in the line-up. As Rufus Knight and Mattie Ligon looked on, Bertucci and Padar walked down the line and manually turned each man to present full face and profile views to the witnesses. Both Rufus Knight and Mattie Ligon positively identified 'the number three man' as the person who had entered, and left, the hotel on the night in question.

Roland Banks phoned Witkowski and told him the result of the line-up.

'Can we book him?' Banks asked.

Witkowski hesitated for a moment. There was a positive 'ident' ... there was what appeared to be blood on Donald's sock. Under ordinary circumstances there would have been little question that the police had sufficient evidence to justify such a move. But Witkowski knew from experience how extraordinary anything concerning Donald Lang could be.

'No,' Witkowski said flatly. 'Release him. Wait for stronger evidence. If that *is* blood on his socks, and *if* the blood matches the victim's, then we can move ahead. But not now.'

Banks passed the word. Bertucci and Padar weren't happy about it. They'd put in a lot of hours on a hot, steamy day and their nerves were getting ragged. They felt that they had more than enough to warrant a formal booking, but Banks was adamant.

'Get his prints and a photo—then let him go home.'

The victim had a name. The prints that Frank Bertucci had taken at the morgue matched prints in the Identification Section files. The report came in early that evening ...

BROWN, Earline F/N, 38 yrs DOB : 5 Sept 1932
LKA :   2629 W. Lexington   No Phone
IR#   39180—record for prostitution

Bertucci's instinct had been correct. Earline Brown had been a West Madison Street hustler.

Donald Lang had been identified by two witnesses as the man who had entered the lobby of the Viceroy Hotel with Earline Brown on Saturday night, 24 July. Lieutenant Azzarello wanted more than that. Someone might have seen Lang or Earline Brown earlier in the evening. He wanted witnesses who could place them together before they went to the hotel.

SUPPLEMENTARY REPORT/CHICAGO POLICE
INVESTIGATION : In the continuance of this investigation the reporting investigators initiated a canvass of the area around the Viceroy Hotel to locate and identify any possible witnesses to this incident ...

Teams of detectives moved into the world of The Bull's Tavern, Johnny Guitar's and Huey's. This was the world that had attracted Donald Lang, that had caused him to leave his turf and seek another. What he had found on West Madison was an abundance of women. Love was for sale on those mean streets, the only kind of love that Donald had ever known. His terrible isolation made it impossible for him to form any other kind of relationship with a woman. He could not whisper sweet nothings into a girl's ear, but he could hold up ten fingers and strike a bargain. His affliction meant nothing to the women who hung around the taverns. They were democratic and tolerant. The halt, the blind, the lame—it didn't matter. They judged a man by the money in his pocket. Donald had no trouble in getting a woman.

Bull was a massive black man weighing close to three hundred pounds. He stood behind the bar in the tavern that bore his name and kept an eye on his customers. He remembered 'the dummy'.

'He'd order a Canadian Club and water and stare at the girls,' Bull said. 'Sometimes he'd write a number on a piece of paper and shove it at one he'd chosen. They'd take him sometimes, charge him like twenty-five dollars for a ten-dollar trick. They were all a little afraid of him, but they took his money. One of them hillbilly girls from Johnny Guitar's came running in here one night, screaming. She didn't have no clothes on, just an old, beat-up bathrobe the manager of the ... I think it was the Viceroy, or maybe the Crest Hotel ... had given her. She said the dummy had slapped her around and run off with her clothes. But she was a trick hustler. I know that for a fact.'

Trick hustling—the favourite sport on the street. A girl could get away with it if she had a good, strong pimp to back up her play. Trick hustling—take the trick's money and run off without performing. If a man was stupid enough, or angry enough, he'd go looking for the girl who had hustled him. Sometimes he'd find her and get his money back, or sometimes he'd find the girl's pimp instead and end up in an alley with a mouth full of loose teeth.

Shirley Thurmond hung out at Bull's. She remembered 'a mute'.

'I saw him with Earline ... Saturday night. Earline was wearing hotpants. She held up ten fingers, you know, meaning ten dollars and the mute nodded his head and they left together. They started off across the street towards the Viceroy and Earline yelled at the bartender that she'd be right back. That was the last time I saw her.'

Detectives typed up their reports and turned them in to Lieutenant Azzarello. It was six-thirty in the morning, Tuesday, 27 July. Nothing further could be done on the case until the blood type reports were received from the crime lab.

Crime reporters had latched on to the story that day. They, too, remembered Donald Lang.

DEAF-MUTE FREED AGAIN IN 2ND BIZARRE MURDER
A 25-year-old deaf-mute, acquitted of a murder charge last February because he could not communicate with his lawyer, was arrested for a second murder—and released again ...

Lowell Myers read the report the next morning and almost dropped the newspaper. It stunned him—and saddened him. He had not seen Donald since the dismissal hearing, but he had hoped that the young man had been on the road to a new life, a better life. Now *this*! It was a terrible shock, brightened only by the report that Donald had been released by the police because of insufficient evidence. He hoped that that would be the end of it, that Donald had just been unlucky enough to be in the vicinity of a crime—but a hard, tight knot had formed in the pit of his stomach.

The crime lab was having difficulty in typing the victim's blood. Cause of death had been determined—asphyxiation, due to external violence applied to the neck and chest. A classic beating—cuts on the face, deep cuts inside the mouth and severe damage to the chest wall and throat. The lab kept working on the blood typing and on Thursday, 29th July they succeeded. Earline Brown's blood was type 'B', a comparatively rare type. The rust-coloured stains on Donald Lang's white sock was determined as being type 'B' blood.

A warrant was issued for the arrest of Donald Lang and at nine o'clock that evening three detectives from Homicide/4 knocked on the door of William and Mary Lang's apartment. Donald was asleep in bed. He would sleep the rest of that night in the Cook County Jail, and all the nights thereafter. There was no bail.

The State moved towards trial and began the slow, painstaking process of gathering evidence. Written depositions were taken from Rufus Knight, Mattie Ligon, Shirley Thurmond and others who said they had seen Donald with Earline Brown on the night of 24 July and the early morning hours of Sunday the 25th. Physical evidence was accumulated bit by bit. It would be a case of circumstantial evidence. No one had seen Donald Lang kill Earline Brown. No one could say that he had threatened her life, by word or gesture. All that the State could prove for a *fact* was that he had left a tavern with her and had walked into a hotel with her. It was a fact that Earline Brown was dead, and it was a fact that blood of her type was on Donald's sock, but the actual event of her death would never, could never be, known.

Blood on the white sock. Then more blood. Donald's step-mother phoned the Maxwell Street station the day after Donald had been taken to jail. She reported that she had found a suit belonging to her son hanging in the back of the clothes closet. A white tee-shirt was with the suit, draped over the pants on the hanger. The tee-shirt was spotted with dried blood.

CHICAGO POLICE DEPARTMENT
CRIMINALISTICS DIVISION
LABORATORY REPORT

On 30 July 1971, Investigator Bertucci, star #3601, submitted articles of clothing identified as being the property of one Donald Lang.

 1 men's brown suit
 1 black men's belt [sic]
 1 men's white tee-shirt with red lettering, (Donald Lang) on collar and tail.

Extracts of dried, reddish-brown stain present on the above articles were subjected to various chemical and serological tests for blood. The results are as follows: The stains tested were found to be composed of human blood, type 'B'.

A search warrant was obtained allowing the police to take a small quantity of blood from Donald Lang so that his blood type could be determined. This was done. His blood type was 'O'.

Blood and more blood. Bloody clothing—bloody sheets—bloody mattress and box spring—vials of blood from victim and suspect—glassine envelopes enclosing bloody hairs. The evidence was carefully filed at the crime lab. There would be no destruction of the evidence in this case.

Lowell Myers was not involved. The day after Donald had been arrested, the Court had asked Myers to represent him. He had turned down the request. The attorney of record was Public Defender Neil Walters. It was his office that would see to it that none of Donald's civil or constitutional rights were violated. There was little else that they could do for him.

The pattern of the first case began to repeat itself. Doctors from the Cook County Behavioural Clinic were called in to examine Donald and their opinion was that he was ... 'emotionally unstable and mentally incompetent to stand trial.' The Public Defender's office moved for a competency hearing. It was 1965 all over again, but with one great difference—the Illinois Supreme Court decision that Lowell Myers had fought so hard to obtain. That ruling was specific—Donald Lang, despite the fact that he was a deaf-mute, had the *right* to a trial. He could not be shunted off to a mental institution. Try the man, the Court had ruled in the earlier case. The ruling would still apply. Try the man, but only an attorney with an intimate knowledge of the deaf world could possibly aid Donald in his defence. Normal, hearing people simply do not understand the unique problems of the deaf. They tend to forget that the sounds they take so much for granted do not exist to the non-hearing. They have trouble grasping the fact that what they say has no meaning. The movement of lips has meaning for a deaf person—if that person can read lips. Donald Lang could not. A non-deaf attorney had permitted the following piece of testimony to be heard before the Cook County Grand Jury. The interrogator was Anthony Montemurro, an Assistant State's Attorney. The man being questioned was Detective Frank Bertucci ...

144

Q. So after the defendant was placed in custody, and of course was advised of his constitutional rights, did he appear to you to understand the nature of his rights?

A. Yes. He was advised on 26 July. At this time we advised him of his constitutional rights.

Q. And subsequently on the 29th?

A. Yes. On the 29th he was re-advised.

Q. And did you advise him by reading the rights to him, and also letting him look at the card with the rights written on there?

A. He was advised both ways, sir.

Myers would have raised an objection at that point. He would have hammered home to the jury that to 'read' Donald his rights and to 'show' Donald his rights were meaningless things, pointless gestures. The State was aware of this. They intended to move for a formal indictment and to bring Donald Lang to trial, but they didn't want a travesty—they wanted, they demanded, Lowell Myers. This time he could not refuse.

CHAPTER XI

STATE OF ILLINOIS } SS.
COUNTY OF COOK }

IN THE CIRCUIT COURT OF COOK COUNTY
COUNTY DEPARTMENT—CRIMINAL DIVISION

THE PEOPLE OF THE ⎫
STATE OF ILLINOIS ⎪ Indictment No. 71-2564
VS ⎬ Charge: Murder
DONALD LANG ⎭

REPORT OF PROCEEDINGS

BE IT REMEMBERED that on the 17th day of January, A.D. 1972, this cause came on for trial before the Honourable EARL E. STRAYHORN, Judge of said court, and a jury, upon the indictment herein, the defendant having entered a plea of not guilty.

APPEARANCES:

HON. EDWARD V. HANRAHAN
    State's Attorney of Cook County, by
MR. ANTHONY P. CORSENTINO,
MR. JOSEPH DiNATALE,
    Assistant State's Attorneys,
    appeared for the people;
MR. LOWELL MYERS, Assisted by:
MRS. JEAN MARKIN
    appeared for the Defendant.

The irony of having the case heard in Judge Strayhorn's court was not lost on Lowell Myers. Fate was strange. It had been almost a year since Donald had sat in this same courtroom at 26th and California Streets. Judge Strayhorn had made him a

146

free man then. Maybe he would again—with a little help from the jury.

Myers felt that he was ready. He had been Donald's counsel since October of the preceding year and he had had ample time to go over the evidence that the State would present. He had spent hours in the crime laboratory while prosecuting attorney Joseph DiNatale stood watching him. There were no shredded bits and pieces of cloth this time. Everything was intact, easy to look at and ponder over. Myers had conceived his defence by looking at blood spots. He had read the rust-coloured markings the way a man might read a book. To Myers, the spots told a story.

So did the Viceroy Hotel. Myers had gone there, too, with his sister Jean Markin, up the creaky stairs to the second floor, down the corridor to Room 201, following the route that Donald Lang and Earline Brown had taken that fateful summer night. He had gone into the small room that had been the scene of so much passion and pain over the years. He looked in the closet, he looked at the bed and peered out of the window. He added what he observed to his argument.

THE COURT : Mr. Myers, are you ready ?

MR. MYERS : Yes, Your Honour.

THE COURT : State ?

MR. CORSENTINO : Yes, Your Honour.

Corsentino and DiNatale would handle the prosecution, with Corsentino making the opening statement and DiNatale the final arguments. They would take turns questioning witnesses. They were a team, and a good one. Their combined experience as prosecutors was enormous, DiNatale alone handling thirty or more cases a year. They were both husky, handsome men who knew how to appeal to a jury. DiNatale was the more flamboyant of the two, a born storyteller, a man who could make a jury laugh—or cry.

Corsentino rose to his feet, standing in such a manner that Myers could read his lips as he spoke. The jury was all white, twelve prosperous-looking men and women. The only black people in the court were the judge and the defendant.

'Good morning, ladies and gentlemen,' Corsentino said, smiling.

'Good morning,' the jury murmured in unison. They seemed a little disgruntled. This was a sequestered jury, in order to prevent them from reading anything in the newspapers about the murder of Ernestine Williams and Donald Lang's involvement in it. The jury on the 'Chicago Seven' conspiracy case had been lodged at the Palmer House. This jury was being quartered at Bridewell, the Cook County misdemeanour farm.

'This trial,' Corsentino began, 'will basically be a recount of certain events that happened beginning with approximately the extremely late evening hours of 24 July 1971, and events that continued until the early morning hours of the 25th, and from the 26th of July 1971 and subsequent police investigations thereto.

'There is an area in the city of Chicago, generally it's around the area of Chicago Stadium where the Black Hawks and the Bulls play. It's approximately the fifteen hundred block on West Madison Street. It's an area teeming with crime, vice, prostitution ...'

He painted a portrait of Donald Lang as a man who, although unable to communicate, was nevertheless a young man with normal sex drives. He was a young man who could not rap with or romance a girl in the normal manner. His affliction had forced him to deal with women on a basic, primitive level. He got his sex the only way he knew how—from prostitutes. He had picked up a prostitute in a tavern called Bull's, and he had gone with this prostitute, one Earline Brown, to the Viceroy Hotel. There, for reasons unknown, he had killed her. Corsentino was taking the jury for a walk on the wild side and he had their complete attention.

'Earline Brown was strangled. She was punched and, or, kicked in the face, stomped on, to use the vernacular. Then Donald Lang did not go out the window that he could have gone out. The room is only on the second floor. There was a roof right below and an open window to that roof, but, instead, the evidence will indicate that he took the bloodstained sheets, he took the bloodstained pillow cases, he took the nearly naked body of Earline Brown and carefully stuffed it in a very small closet ... he also stuffed her ripped clothing in that closet with the body. He then took the mattress and overturned it so the blood did not show. He was very careful, very methodical and approximately one hour after they entered that room, Donald Lang was seen coming out of there. Earline Brown was not seen after that.'

Corsentino talked about the blood, the type 'B' blood, that had been found on Donald's white tee-shirt and on his pants.

Earline Brown's blood was type 'B'. Donald's was type 'O'.

'So, therefore, ladies and gentlemen,' Corsentino said, wrapping it up, 'what remains is for us to stop talking, to present you with this evidence, circumstantial evidence. And then we ask you not to make up your mind now or even during the course of the evidence. Just listen and we assure you that it will all fall together.'

It was Lowell Myers' turn. This was a case based strictly on circumstantial evidence—the State had nothing more, and Myers knew it. Jury impression was vital. It was the key to the case. They would weigh the evidence presented by the State against their impression of the defendant. Myers could not dispute the fact that Donald had picked up, or been picked up by, Earline Brown. He could not dispute the fact that people had seen them walk out of The Bull's Tavern, or that other people had seen them walk into the Viceroy Hotel. That was a matter of record and Myers had no intention of denying it. What he intended to prove to the jury was that Donald had done nothing more than have sex with a prostitute. That was his only 'crime'. What other events took place in that room at the Viceroy Hotel were not of Donald's doing. The woman had been murdered, she had not beaten herself to death and stuffed her own body in a closet. She had been killed—and Donald had been a silent witness to that killing. Those were the bare bones of his defence, and the credibility of it depended greatly on the jury's impression of Donald Lang. And that impression was of some concern to Myers.

Donald had been in the County Jail since 30 July 1971— nearly six months. He appeared in court looking sullen and bitter. He was restless and terribly tense. Myers glanced at him before making his opening address and he looked like a man on the verge of exploding. Something was bothering him, but Myers had no clue to what it might be.

'Ladies and gentlemen of the jury, as you all know, my name is Lowell Myers and I represent Donald Lang who is the defendant in this case ...'

Myers began by recounting the extent of Donald's disability. He was a man with aphasia and he could neither read nor write nor speak. To counter any claim by the police that he could hear, write and read, Myers explained that Donald could say certain words. He could say 'home' and 'water' and he knew, for some reason, the word 'finished'. But other than those few words he could say nothing. He could read his own name—if it were written in very large block letters; he could read the word BUDWEISER and the words COCA COLA; but other than those words, he could read nothing. He could write a few letters down. He could begin to write his own name but was incapable of completing it. Four, or at the most five, letters in consecutive order was the extent of his writing ability.

Myers then told of Donald's background of work, how he loaded and unloaded trucks and how good he was at his job. Donald, he said, was a young man who worked for a living and went home at night, to an apartment that he shared with his father and his stepmother. And, like most young men who worked all week and made good money, he went out on Saturday night. He put on a good suit of clothes and went out with money in his pocket, to buy a few drinks—and to have the pleasure of a woman. The only type of women that Donald could have pleasure with were prostitutes. Donald met a prostitute in The Bull's Tavern. They struck a bargain—ten fingers—ten dollars—and they left the tavern and walked to the Viceroy Hotel.

'Let's talk about the hotel. This hotel is used by prostitutes and it is used by people who sell drugs. This woman took Donald into the hotel and Donald paid for a room. And as they walked through the lobby, there was a man there. And this man knew the woman. He had seen her come into the hotel many times with different men and he recognized her. And it so happens that this man has known Donald Lang since Donald was a little boy, it just happened that way. And Donald waved to the man and the man waved back. And Donald and the woman went up to Room 201.

'Now, the hotel becomes very important. This hotel has six floors and on every floor there are twenty rooms. There are more than one hundred rooms in this hotel and most of those rooms were occupied. There are stairways in this hotel going to every floor ... anybody on one floor can go to another floor. In this hotel there are twelve janitors and maids and people working in the building. All of these people have passkeys. And the people who work there come and go. And sometimes when they go, they take a passkey with them. It is very simple to duplicate a key.

'Now, Donald and the woman went up to Room 201 on the second floor and it's close to the stairway in the front of the building. They had sexual relations in that room. We know that because sperm was found inside of the woman. They were done having sexual relations and they were just about to leave the room when three men came into that room. Now, this is what Donald communicated to the policemen at the police station when he was arrested the following day, that *three men came into that room.*'

The prosecuting attorneys shifted slightly in their seats. DiNatale doodled on a piece of paper. Corsentino's face was impassive. This, then, was the crux of Myers' defensive strategy ... three men.

'Now,' Myers continued, 'this is something that we must consider very carefully because Donald was there and he knows what happened. The evidence will show that one of the men took Donald and put him down on the floor in the middle of the room. Another man took the woman and he started to argue with her and he started to fight with her. This woman was strong. A well-developed, husky woman. This woman had been in many fights in her lifetime. There is blood underneath all of the woman's fingernails and there was a terrific fight in this room. This fight went from the front of the room to the back wall and it went from one side wall to the other side wall. The woman was hit in the face repeatedly and she was bleeding profusely. Blood was dropping all over the room—everywhere. And the bloodstains are still there right now because they had not changed the carpeting and there are bloodstains in the front of the room, the back of the room, and both sides of the room, but there are no bloodstains in one particular place, right in the middle.'

'Now, this woman was bleeding from the face and the man was hitting her repeatedly very hard and when the man's fists hit her face, some of the blood was spattered. And when small drops of blood fly through the air, they become perfectly round. And when those small, round drops of blood hit something, they make a perfectly small circle—small, but perfectly round. Now, one of those small, flying drops of blood fell on top of Donald and it fell on the *seat* of his pants. At that time, Donald was on the floor with his face down and the seat of his pants upwards.

'And all this time the man and the woman are fighting, and eventually the man got this woman down on the bed and he started to strangle her, and the woman was struggling and fighting and it took a long time. And all that time, the woman was bleeding and bleeding and bleeding. And there was a puddle, a pool of blood on the bed, and the sheets on the bed are simply soaked in blood. And the puddle of blood went through into the mattress and the mattress is soaked, too. This man was right in the middle of this puddle of blood—he was on top of the woman in all that blood.

'Now, Donald's clothes show a few, very small blood marks, but there are no heavy bloodstains on any of Donald's clothes, nothing. After the man left, after he had taken her purse and ripped out the lining, we do not know exactly what Donald did, but he eventually left the room and he walked down into the lobby. He went straight to the telephone in the lobby and took the telephone off the hook and he looked at it for a minute and then he put it back. He then went out of the hotel and he went home. He got home at three-thirty in the morning and he went to sleep. And the next day, Monday, he went to work just like he always goes to work.

'Donald did not report this to the police, but Donald can't communicate and he can't speak. When they arrested Donald, there were no scratches on his face of any kind. And at the time Donald was in that hotel, he was wearing a thin, white tee-shirt. It was not torn. It was not ripped.

'The police took Donald to a police station and they took a look at him and they saw that there was a bloodstain on his stocking and Donald saw them looking at his stocking and he tried to cover it up. Then the police gave Donald a paper and pencil and Donald drew a picture, and he made motions as he tried to explain that three men had killed the woman. Now, he did not communicate too well, but for Donald, this was brilliant because Donald usually does not communicate at all. The policemen did not understand Donald. They have never met a person like Donald before and he was arrested for murder and he is now sitting in that chair. Donald was in the room at the time the woman was killed. There are small, minor bloodstains on his clothes and that is the woman's blood, but we will prove that he is not the man who killed her. Thank you.'

Judge Strayhorn glanced at the clock. 'All right. We will recess for lunch, opening statements of counsel having been completed.'

The jury was led out by the bailiffs, the prosecutors made notes on long pads of yellow paper, and Donald Lang was removed from the courtroom by Deputy Sheriff Joseph Galati to the bull-pen, a small lock-up cell outside the courtroom where prisoners on trial were kept between sessions. Joseph Galati would testify during the course of the trial that he had no trouble handling the defendant. He would give him a cigarette if he seemed distraught, or a piece of candy. Joseph Galati, in his own simple way, communicated very well with Donald Lang.

In the first stage of a murder trial the crime is broadly sketched for the benefit of the jury and the ground rules are laid out between attorneys. Lowell Myers was concerned over the fact that a number of police officers would be called to testify for the prosecution. Before the jury was brought in for that first afternoon's session, he asked for a ruling on a motion and approached the Bench flanked by Corsentino and DiNatale.

'Your Honour,' Myers said. 'I have a motion. Some of the policemen that may be called by the State may have worked upon the previous case which involved the defendant. And so I would like to have an order that the prosecutor shall instruct his witnesses before they testify that they must not refer to any previous case because that could lead to a mistrial.'

'Sustained,' Judge Strayhorn said.

The scene was set, the jury led by the hand into a world alien to their own, a world of vice and drugs and crime. John Cello, a sergeant with the Chicago Police, answered questions put to him by Anthony Corsentino in a matter-of-fact manner, just a man talking about his job ...

Q. Sergeant Cello, as a vice officer, what particular areas of criminal activity were you concentrating on?

A. Prostitution, gambling, narcotics.

Q. Sergeant, as a vice officer, were you aware of any particular categories or classifications of prostitution?

A. Streetwalkers and call girls.

Q. How does the streetwalker meet her, shall we say, customer?

A. Usually on the street, doorways, gangways, parking lots, taverns, anything along the street where they can meet.

Q. All right. And where do they go with their customers?

A. They will go either to a rooming house, hotel, automobile, parked cars. They have been known to use hallways, gangways, alleys. A lot of them have mattresses set up on their porch during the summer. Just about anywhere.

Q. Do streetwalkers generally, shall we say, entertain one customer a night?

A. No, they entertain on an average of anywhere from ten to twenty, depends on how hard the person wants to work.

Q. During your course of employment as a vice officer, did you have occasion to come to know one Earline Brown?

A. Yes, I did. She was a prostitute—a streetwalker.

Q. Sergeant Cello, is there any other criminal activity related to or comes as an offshoot of streetwalking?

A. Yes, it leads into many other activities such as robbery, strongarm robbery ... and 'rip off'. 'Rip off' is the same as the term 'burn' ... it's where a prostitute will take a man into a rooming house say, or an hotel room, accept the money and say, I will be right back, I have to get a towel or something, and she will walk out, leave the man stranded in the room and take off with the money.

Lowell Myers had no questions. The background helped his case as much as it helped the State's. The next witness to 'set the scene' was Shirley Thurmond, also known as Shirley Wilson and by four or five other names. She was a thin, still pretty black woman, age twenty-six, occupation, prostitute.

She was a reluctant witness who appeared in court with an attorney, Public Defender Alan Jacobs. She had requested immunity from prosecution for testifying that she was a working streetwalker. The Court granted that immunity, but her attitude on the stand was one of sullen resentment, especially towards Anthony Corsentino. Corsentino had been a cop before he became an attorney. He had arrested Shirley Thurmond in 1966 and his testimony in court had been instrumental in sending her to jail. She did not like Corsentino in any way and her eyes showed it.

Q. What is your business, profession or occupation?

A. Streetwalker.

Q. You will have to speak up. The jury wants to hear you.

A. I am a streetwalker!

Q. How long have you been so employed?

A. Six years.

Q. All right. Calling your attention to the night of the 24th of July, approximately eleven-thirty p.m., do you remember where you were at that time?

A. I was over on the West Side, Madison ... I was in a tavern ... name of Bull's Tavern.

Q. What were you doing in that tavern?

A. Hustling.

Q. Explain to the jury what 'hustling' means.

A. I was prostituting.

Shirley Thurmond's tone of voice became progressively sharper as Corsentino forced her to spell out for the jury precisely how she made her living. Was she trying to pick up customers at the tavern? Yes. Would she engage in prostitution with the customers? Yes. For money? Yes.

Q. And was there any going rate for your favours?

A. I don't know what you mean by rates.

Q. Well, let me re-phrase the question for you. Would you ever go up to a room with a customer for just three dollars?

A. No.

Lowell Myers made his own notations on a legal-size pad. It was easy to see what the State was digging for. When Donald had held up three fingers in the police station, Myers had interpreted the gesture to mean *three men*. The State would probably try to prove that the three fingers had meant *three dollars*. Myers glanced at the jury. They were totally absorbed by the life-style of the witness.

Q. Did you state that you had been in The Bull's Tavern that Saturday night and that Earline Brown and other girls were in there with yourself and that a man whom you knew only as 'the mute' was in the tavern bothering the girls and that on one occasion, the mute came up to you and rubbed your knee? And did you also state that later you saw the mute trying to communicate with Earline Brown? And did you further state that you saw the victim show the mute ten fingers, meaning ten dollars, and that the mute nodded his head up and down and that shortly thereafter, between twelve-thirty a.m. and one a.m. on Sunday, the 25th of July 1971, you saw Earline Brown in the company of the mute leave the tavern and go across the street northbound on Ogden towards Warren Boulevard?

A. Are you through?

Q. Yes.

A. Yes.

A hard witness, every answer dragged out of her, but she served her purpose. She established that Earline Brown, one of the sisterhood of West Madison Street, had met 'the mute' in the tavern and had walked out with him. The chain of events that would lead Donald Lang and Earline Brown to Room 201 of the Viceroy Hotel would be followed, link by link over the next two days.

There was Mattie Ligon, resident manager of the hotel. She had been on duty behind the desk when the couple entered. The man she identified as Donald Lang had slipped a five dollar bill across the counter and she had turned away to make change. No, she did not see whether or not the man had filled out the registry card. When she turned back with the change, the card had been filled out. Yes, the woman could have done it.

Rufus Knight had seen the couple enter. The front door was locked. They had rung the bell and Mrs. Ligon had pressed a buzzer that activated the lock. The couple had walked into the lobby and crossed to the desk. Rufus Knight had recognized Donald Lang, had given him the high sign and Donald had waved back.

The night maid, Sarah Williams, age seventy-five, testified about going to the room and finding the sheets missing. No, she hadn't heard any sounds of an argument on the second floor during the time the couple were in Room 201. She had been making up a room directly across the hall ...

A. Well, I didn't hear any screaming from that room. But when I was going to 200 to make that bed, I could hear somebody, wasn't no screaming, just a little mumbling like somebody might have been talking, not enough for me to pay any attention.

Q. While you were making your rounds, did you observe any groups of people, men or women, leaving together from 201 or going into 201?

A. I don't recall seeing anyone. No group.

Joseph DiNatale was questioning Sarah Williams, and he questioned her at great length about the condition of Room 201 when she went in there to put new sheets on the bed.

Q. Did you have an opportunity to examine any of the walls next to the bed?

A. I did.

Q. Did you observe anything unusual about the walls?

A. I saw a little spot. Wasn't unusual.

Q. And what colour was that spot?
A. It was red.
Q. And did you see any other spots?
A. I saw a little pinkish spot on the floor by the dresser.
Q. Now, as you looked at the carpet, did you see anything unusual about the carpet itself?
A. Not nothing unusual. Just a dirty carpet.

Lowell Myers cross-examined the maid. Myers had noticed on his visit to the hotel early in November that the room had been freshly painted and the carpet cleaned. But he had noticed spots on that carpet.

Q. Was the carpet cleaned before we went up to look at the room or was the carpet cleaned afterwards?
A. It was cleaned—let's see. It was cleaned before you all went up.
Q. They didn't clean it very good, did they?
A. It was just a bad carpet.
Q. It is still pretty dirty, isn't it?
A. Yes.

The parade of witnesses continued, each one adding little bits and pieces to the mosaic of the case. There was the young woman who had discovered the body, and the hotel janitor she had called. There were the uniformed officers who had first appeared on the scene, and the men from the mobile crime lab unit who had taken the body out of the closet. The jury listened patiently, silent in their own thoughts.

Donald Lang was not so patient, nor so silent. He was becoming something of a problem and very much of a worry to Lowell Myers. During the competency hearings, Donald had been bored and a little restless at times, but usually he had appeared relaxed and friendly. Not so now. He slouched in his chair and glowered at the jury and the prosecuting attorneys. Sometimes, when he was in the bull pen before Sheriff Galati brought him into the courtroom, the jury could hear Donald howling and screaming. Donald was unable to hear the sound of his own voice and thus was unable to regulate it. When he was disturbed or agitated in any way, his voice would often rise like the wail of a fire siren. It was disconcerting to Myers and he worried about its effect on the jury. There was no way he could gauge that effect and nothing he could do about it, other than hope that Donald would calm down.

Long after the trial was over, Nathaniel Brown, a warden

at Cook County Jail, reported that he suspected Donald was being antagonized by someone while he was in the bull pen during the trial. Brown assigned one of the prison guards to go with Donald to see that he was left alone.

Witnesses for the State continued to appear—laboratory technicians, doctors from the Coroner's office, a forensic micro-analyst, even a spectroscopist with experience in laser excitation procedures—minute particles of green paint had been found on Donald's clothes and on the clothing of Earline Brown. The State made an issue of this discovery and asked the spectroscopist to explain at great length the procedures involved in testing the composition of such infinitesimal particles. There was, the State added darkly, no green paint anywhere in Room 201, no green paint anywhere in the Viceroy Hotel. The significance of the paint was not explained (no one had examined the interior of Bull's Tavern to see if there was green paint there) but Myers raised no objections. He simply jotted down a few notes for future reference.

Detective James Padar was called to the stand and questioned by Corsentino. Padar recounted his lengthy role in the investigation and his testimony was uneventful, merely the minute-by-minute mechanics of working a murder case.

Q. Investigator Padar, while you were in Room 201 on the afternoon of the 26th of July, did you or anybody in your presence move any furniture in addition to the bed?

A. Yes, sir. I believe there was a chair that was moved in order to make room for the movement of the body from the closet.

Q. Was there a chest in that room?

A. Yes, sir.

Q. Was that moved?

A. Not to my knowledge, sir.

And then Corsentino asked a question that was completely non sequitur. The question was so unexpected at that point in Padar's testimony that he answered it without thinking ...

Q. By the way, did you make a determination as to the age of the defendant, Donald Lang?

A. Yes, sir, according to the police records ...

Judge Strayhorn nearly jumped out of his seat. 'Strike that! The jury is instructed to disregard it. Wipe it completely out of your minds.'

'I'm sorry, Your Honour,' Padar said.

'You know better than that,' Strayhorn said sharply. 'The next time, I'm going to take stringent action!'

'Yes, sir,' Padar murmured.

Corsentino paused for a moment and then continued.

'What was the age of the defendant, officer?'

'We determined his age to be twenty-five years, sir.'

Strayhorn was fuming and getting angrier by the second. He slapped his gavel down and looked over at the jury.

'The jury is instructed to disregard any statement that this officer made about *"according to police records"*. I want you to wipe it out of your minds completely. We will have a short recess ... take the jury out.'

The jury filed out of the courtroom while Officer Padar shifted uncomfortably in his chair. Judge Strayhorn fixed him with a hard, cold stare.

'Officer Padar, I ought to write a letter to the Superintendent of Police. If there is a mistrial in this case ... I am going to attribute it to you because you have caused a mistrial. You have put a prejudicial air, or what *could* be a very serious prejudicial air, into this case which up to this time we have successfully kept out. And from now on, whenever you come into a courtroom that has the name Strayhorn on it, you will confine your answers and your testifying to that which you know and you will not add anything or subtract anything. Do I make myself clear to you?'

'Yes, sir,' Padar replied miserably.

Corsentino hurried to offer explanations, but the judge would have none of it. He waved Corsentino away.

'I don't want to hear it. He knew better than that. We have succeeded up to this time. This jury had no knowledge of any police records on the part of this man. They don't need to have any. This is a hard enough case as it is. This is a purely circumstantial evidence case. You know that.'

'Yes, Judge.'

'Circumstantial evidence ... so how can you say ... how can anyone say if this jury goes out and returns a verdict of guilty, what caused them to come to that conclusion. So don't give me any excuses for this officer. Now, get him out of my sight and let me cool off.'

'Might I suggest a recess?'

'We're having a recess right now! We are going to continue this case.'

But first, Lowell Myers made a motion before the Bench ...

'Your Honour, the fact is that Donald Lang has never been found guilty of anything in his lifetime, not even a parking ticket. He has been arrested previously, but there was no conviction. However, the jury has been given the worst possible impression and they may think he's a confirmed convict. Now, the Court has done a beautiful job of trying to instruct the jury to disregard that remark of Officer Padar, but no human being can forget something of that character. The more discussion there is on the matter, the more sure it is that they are bound to think about it. Merely to refer to it is to emphasize it. I believe that on behalf of the defendant, it is my duty to move for a mistrial.

Judge Strayhorn thought over the proposal carefully. It was his opinion, now that his temper had cooled somewhat, that the remark was not of sufficient magnitude to declare a mistrial. The jury had been instructed to disregard the remark and Corsentino and DiNatale were more than willing to stipulate before the jury that Donald Lang had never been convicted of any crime either in the State of Illinois or anywhere else. This was satisfactory to Myers and the jury was called back. Before court recessed for the day, DiNatale read the stipulation for the jury and for the record.

CHAPTER XII

Thursday, 20 January 1972. Donald Lang was brought up from the County Jail in the morning and placed in the bull pen outside the courtroom. He was in an extremely agitated state. Lowell Myers tried to calm him down but Donald only seemed to get worse. He moved back and forth in the lock-up like a caged animal, mouth open, emitting ear-piercing howls. Myers was worried about bringing him into court in such a state. It was bound to frighten the jury and could have a catastrophic effect. Fortunately, Donald stopped screaming before court was called into session, but Myers had grave misgivings. Donald was momentarily silent, but he seemed far from calm. When the sheriff brought him into the courtroom, Donald sank into his chair and glared broodingly at his surroundings.

'The People of the State of Illinois versus Donald Lang,' the clerk intoned.

'Mr. Myers, are you ready?' Judge Strayhorn asked.

'Your Honour,' Myers said, 'I think I'm going to make a motion. The defendant seems to be losing patience. I am going to argue that we should proceed without him being present. He does not contribute anything. He does not hear anything. I think we should continue without him.'

The strangest murder trial in the history of the United States had just been given an added twist.

Anthony Corsentino objected. 'Your Honour, he is the *defendant*!'

'Your Honour,' Myers said. 'We do not wish to have a mistrial in this case due to his behaviour.'

Judge Strayhorn had heard the mêlée in the lock-up area as he sat in chambers. He eyed Donald carefully and could see for himself that there was bound to be another outburst. Donald was getting agitated again, turning and twisting in his chair. 'Take him back.'

Veteran court reporters scribbled furiously on their pads, There would be headlines in the Chicago papers the next day ...

DEAF-MUTE EXCUSED FROM ATTENDING HIS MURDER TRIAL cried the *Sun-Times*.

HE'LL SKIP HIS OWN MURDER TRIAL said *Chicago-Today*.

Corsentino and DiNatale shook their heads. There had never been a murder trial in the history of Cook County where the defendant had not been present. It was bizarre.

Officer Frank Bertucci was the next witness for the State. Like Officer Padar, he recounted his role in the investigation of Donald Lang. He stuck to the facts and only at one point did he swerve into the area of opinion.

Q. Officer Bertucci, did you have occasion as a result of your conference with Mrs. Lang, to further investigate the educational and hospital, if any, background of Donald Lang?

A. Yes, sir, I did.

Q. Were you able to find out any information with regard to the handicap of Donald Lang?

A. Yes, sir. I was able to obtain a photocopy of a letter written regarding the case of Donald Lang. It showed that he had been taught to lip read, but had never completely mastered the subject.

Myers bided his time. He waited until DiNatale was finished with the witness, then he rose to cross-examine.

Q. Did you read the letter?

A. Yes, I did, sir.

Q. And it said he had been taught lip reading but he never mastered it?

A. Never completely mastered it. Right, sir.

Q. Didn't the letter say that he *never* mastered it?

A. That is correct, sir. He never completely mastered it.

Q. Doesn't the letter state that although Donald was taught to read lips in school, he has never mastered the skill and is unable to vocalize other than to the extent of saying *mama* and *bye-bye*?

A. That is correct, sir.

Q. It doesn't say anything about *completely*, does it?

A. I am going according to the best of my recollection, sir.

Q. Do you think Donald can read lips?

A. My personal opinion, sir?

162

Q. Yes, your personal opinion.

A. My personal opinion is that he can *hear* and read lips.

They brought Donald back into court for the afternoon session. He was quiet, but bored. He slumped low in his chair, legs spread out in front of him, and he alternately yawned and glowered at the prosecuting attorneys. The afternoon session would be a long one and Myers kept his fingers crossed. If only Donald would fall asleep—the jury couldn't fault him for that. It was the screaming that bothered Myers. If Donald started to act up in court all that DiNatale or Corsentino had to do was to raise an eyebrow. It would be like saying to the jury ... *See? This man is a wild man ... a beast.*

Timothy J. Zamb was called. Zamb was a forensic microanalyst who had worked in the police department crime lab for five years. He held a bachelor's degree in biology and was working towards his master's. He was an expert on blood typing and on the microscopic analysis of hair fragments and other substances. DiNatale questioned him about every object and piece of evidence that had been turned over to the lab. DiNatale laid particular stress on the blood that had been found under the victim's fingernails. There had been minute quantities of human blood under all of her nails, but the amount had been insufficient for Zamb to determine whether the blood was type 'B' or 'O'—there was no way to tell. There had been fibres mixed in with the blood and Zamb had been able to analyse them. They were not of human origin, not skin or hair, but cloth, microscopic pieces of lint.

The questioning of Zamb went on for hours as DiNatale brought out every scrap of evidence that the State had accumulated.

Q. And calling your attention to 32-B, C and D ... did you have occasion to take any part of those exhibits and do anything with them?

A. Yes, sir. I made cutouts of the wrappers. These cutouts were of reddish-brown stains present on each of the wrappers.

Q. Those being the white paper of the chewing gum wrappers, Wrigley's spearmint gum?

A. That is correct.

The jury began to fidget in their chairs as the testimony went on and on. Towards the close of his examination of the witness DiNatale probed for one of the most important points of all— the bloodstains on Donald's pants.

Q. Would you turn the pants over and tell us whether or not you were able to find any portions of blood or reddish-brown substance on the back of those pants?

A. There are various stains present on the rear panels, but these tested negative for blood.

Q. How did they test on the front part of the pants?

A. They tested positive for blood.

This was an essential part of Myers' defence. When at last DiNatale was through, Myers jumped immediately to the point.

Q. I want to ask you about the pants, Mr. Zamb. On the front of these pants is a red circle, and inside the red circle, there are some very small, round, reddish-brown marks.

A. Yes, sir.

Q. I would like you to look at them and give us your expert opinion whether you think they were caused by flying drops of blood. By flying drops of blood, I mean little pieces of blood that flew through the air before they hit the cloth.

A. The deposits in my opinion were not caused by contact or smearing. The origin, or source, of blood was a distance away from the trousers.

Q. Some distance away?

A. Yes, sir. They were not, in other words, in contact with the source of blood if that is what you're asking.

It was precisely what Lowell Myers was asking. He had, he felt, scored an important point. *Flying* drops of blood had landed on Donald's brown pants—in the front. The bloodstains on the back were another matter. In fact, Zamb had said flatly that there was no blood on the rear panels.

Q. There is a circle on the back of the trousers. Would you look at that one and tell us in your opinion if that is a flying drop of blood?

A. No, sir, it isn't. The material cannot be characterized as human blood due to the quantity.

Q. So, from your test, you couldn't tell, is that right?

A. That is correct.

Q. Just by looking ... could you form an opinion?

A. By visual examination, it would indicate that it is a bloodstain, but I can't tell the origin of that particular stain.

Q. Your own personal opinion is that it is blood, but you can't tell whether it is human or not?

A. That is correct.

Myers walked slowly back to the attorneys' table and glanced down at his notepad, allowing a little time for Timothy J. Zamb's opinion to sink into the minds of the jurors.

Q. Mr. Zamb, you testified earlier that you examined a pair of lady's sandals, State's exhibits 19-C and 19-D. These sandals were identified as belonging to the lady who was killed, and I see there is a lot of blood on them.

A. Yes, sir, there is.

Q. Now, did you examine the dried human blood and did you find something embedded in that dried blood on the sandals?

A. Yes, sir, medium-brown, human hair.

Q. Did you have a sample of human hair that was identified as belonging to the dead lady?

A. Yes, sir.

Q. And what colour was it?

A. Black to grey.

Q. Did you compare this hair with the sample of hair found on the sandals?

A. Yes, sir.

Q. Were they the same?

A. No, sir, they were not.

Q. Do you have a sample of Donald's hair?

A. No, sir.

Myers stepped away from the witness and asked for a pair of scissors. Paper shears were found and Myers snipped some hair from the top of Donald's head and placed the black, curly strands in Mr. Zamb's palm.

'I want you to examine these strands. Do it overnight and come back tomorrow.' He turned towards the Bench. 'I'm going to make this man my own witness. I want him to testify.'

There was an objection to Myers' move by Corsentino, but Judge Strayhorn overruled him.

'Is that sufficient, Mr. Zamb, to make a comparison?' Myers asked.

Timothy J. Zamb peered at the loose strands of hair in his palm.

'I can indicate right now just by looking at them that there is a difference in the width and colouration.'

'No,' Judge Strayhorn cut in. 'Examine them microscopically so that you can be positive. Give the man an envelope to keep them in.'

The witness was excused and Myers sat down. He had made a point or two—and Donald had been very quiet. All in all, it had been a good afternoon.

Myers had not expected any controversy over whether or not Donald could hear or speak. He felt, rightly enough, that that issue had been settled years before. But Officer Bertucci had raised a doubt in the minds of the jury. Bertucci had merely expressed an opinion, but he was a policeman, a detective, and his opinion would not be taken lightly. The State pressed their attack on the credibility of Donald's affliction. If the defendant was not totally deaf and dumb, if he could communicate in some meaningful manner, the ramifications of such a disclosure would be devastating to Myers' case. If Donald could speak then he could have called for help when the woman was attacked by three men, as Myers claimed she had been. Or if Donald knew sign language, he could have reported the incident to the police. Corsentino placed Phillip Murphy on the stand.

Phillip Murphy was thirty-eight years old. He had been a Chicago police officer for twelve years, attached to Area 5 Robbery. He was an expert in dactology, the art of sign language, having been taught the skill by his deaf-mute parents when he was three years old. He was often called into cases involving deaf-mutes to act as their interpreter. He had first met Donald Lang shortly after Donald's arrest the previous July. Judge Olson of the circuit court had asked him to try and communicate with Donald.

Q. How many times did you meet with Donald Lang over the period of last summer?

A. Three times.

Q. During that period of time were you able to communicate with him in sign language?

A. Yes, I was. Minimally.

Q. Did you ask him his name?

A. Yes, I did.

Q. Did he give a reply?

A. Verbally, yes. In his high-pitched manner, he said ...
Lang. He said Lang is the last name.

Q. Did you ask him that question by use of your mouth or
by use of sign language?

A. Both.

Q. Officer, based on your vast experience in the use of sign
language and also based on your observation and contact with
Donald Lang, do you have an opinion as to whether or not
Donald Lang can understand, at least minimally, sign language?

A. I think it's a combination of lip reading and sign language.

Q. And on these occasions you were able to communicate
with him at least minimally?

A. Yes.

'Mr. Myers,' Corsentino said, 'your witness.'

Myers was tightlipped as he approached the witness. He
looked at Officer Murphy for a long moment, then said:

'When did you first meet him?'

'August ... some time last August.'

'How long were you with him?'

'Half an hour.'

'And the second time?'

'Fifteen minutes.'

'And the third time?'

Officer Murphy pursed his lips and thought about it. 'I think
it was two months ago.'

'And how long was that visit?'

'Well, I didn't speak to him at that point.'

'You tried to communicate with him twice, not three times?'

'Yes,' Officer Murphy said. 'Twice.'

'Why did you say three times?' Myers asked sharply.

Corsentino objected to the form of the question and the
objection was sustained.

'All right,' Myers said. 'You were with him for thirty minutes the first time ... what words did he communicate to you
besides the word *Lang*? I'd like a list of them.'

'Well ... a few other things that we asked him. I was there
in an interpreter's capacity, not a police officer's capacity.'

'That wasn't the question. I said *what words did he communicate to you*? I want a list of them!'

'His name ... his age ... I don't recall.'

Myers looked incredulous. 'He told you his age?'

Officer Murphy appeared uncomfortable. 'I don't recall his age. But I asked him what his age was.'

'And what was his reply?'

'I don't recall.'

'You don't recall?'

'No, sir.'

'You said earlier that you could communicate with Donald minimally, is that correct?'

'Yes, sir.'

'You can communicate with a *dog* minimally, can't you?'

Another objection was raised. The suppressed anger of Lowell Myers was obvious. Again the objection was sustained and Myers refrained from further sarcasm. The balance of his questioning was more gentle. Murphy understood the deaf-mute world very well. He concurred with Myers on many points, especially on the uncanny ability of deaf-mutes to sense what was going on around them by watching people's eyes or facial expressions. They were exceptionally sensitive people who lived in a strange world and they often did things that could lead non-handicapped persons to erroneous conclusions.

'No further questions,' Myers said.

It was now late in the afternoon and Judge Strayhorn recessed the proceedings until the following day.

The trial was moving towards its close. The major witnesses for the State had all been heard. The physical evidence had been compiled. It was Myers' opportunity to bring out witnesses for the defence. They would be mainly character witnesses—Donald's father, stepmother, brothers and sister, Mario Pullano; people who had known the defendant over a period of many years. But first Myers called Timothy Zamb to tell the jury the result of his test on the hairs found on the victim's sandals. Under microscopic examination, the hairs were judged to be totally dissimilar to Donald Lang's hair, or the victim's. The hairs were long, silky, light brown in colour, probably from a caucasian individual.

DiNatale cross-examined. He accepted the fact that the hairs were not Donald's nor Earline Brown's, but he offered a solution as to how they got on the sandals.

Q. I don't mean to embarrass you, Mr. Zamb, but are you married or single?

A. I am single.

Q. Do you remember talking to my associate, Mr. Corsentino, in the hall this morning?

A. Yes, sir.

Q. Now, at the time Mr. Corsentino talked to you, didn't he make some comment to you about a hair particle which was on your suit coat?

A. Yes, sir, he did.

Q. And that particle is still on your coat, isn't it? Do you know how it came to be there?

A. No, sir.

Q. But you do have a pretty good idea, don't you?

A. I might ... yes, sir.

The young microanalyst blushed and the jury smiled. Di-Natale did not have to elaborate. He was inferring that if hairs from an unknown source could drift on to a man's coat, then they could also drift on to a woman's sandal. Myers said nothing in rebuttal. He could not disprove the assumption of counsel and he would withhold his comments for the final argument.

Did any members of the jury have lingering doubts as to Donald's inability to speak or hear? It was possible, and any such doubts had to be laid to rest. It was imperative that the jury understand the totality of Donald's affliction, and so the final witnesses that Myers brought into court were people who would illustrate the silence and frustration of Donald's world. He brought the deaf and the dumb.

Mary Frances Mulcrone acted as interpreter. Mrs. Mulcrone's parents had been deaf-mutes and she had worked with the deaf for many years, teaching sign language and lip reading and acting as an interpreter for many government agencies. As the various deaf-mute witnesses took the stand, Mrs. Mulcrone translated oral questions into sign language. The witnesses answered in sign language and Mrs. Mulcrone translated the signs into English. The jurors were fascinated.

'How many years of experience have you had working with deaf-mute people?' Myers asked a Mr. John B. Davis.

Mary Mulcrone's hands moved through the complicated gestures of sign language. John Davis answered her with lightning movements of his own. It was very quiet in the courtroom as everyone watched this silent communication.

'Over forty years,' Mrs. Mulcrone said. 'For the past seven years, he has been president of the Illinois Association of the Deaf.'

'Did you ever meet Donald Lang before 25 July 1971?' Myers asked.

Again there was a flash of fingers as Mary Mulcrone passed on Myers' question and John Davis answered.

'Yes, twice,' Mary Mulcrone said.

John Davis had met Donald at the Jewish Vocational Centre. He had been unable to communicate with him in any way.

'He just stared at me and tried to talk like a hearing person.'

Mary Mulcrone translated for the remaining witnesses. Jerry Strom, an officer with the National Fraternal Society of the Deaf had also met Donald Lang.

'In your opinion, Mr. Strom, is Donald Lang a deaf-mute?'

A moment of silence—a flutter of hands—and then Mary Mulcrone said:

'Obviously.'

'Does he know sign language?'

'No.'

'Do you think he can read or write?'

'No.'

'Could you communicate with him about the past?'

'I could not.'

'Do you think anyone in the United States could do it?'

'I do not think anyone could.'

Katie Brown was the final deaf witness. She told of her first meeting with Donald at the Ephatha Evangelical Lutheran Church. No, she had never been able to communicate with Donald in all the eleven years she had known him. No, she had never seen him draw anything or communicate in any way. She had found him to be unteachable—although she had tried by every means she knew.

Myers felt sure that the jurors had gained an understanding of the difficulties faced by deaf-mute people. The men and the women he had brought to the stand could at least communicate with their own. Donald was doubly cursed. His silence and his aloneness were absolute.

'The defence rests, Your Honour,' Myers said.

Judge Strayhorn nodded in satisfaction and looked over at the jury.

'You will be delighted to know, ladies and gentlemen,

that both sides have rested on their case in chief, and this matter will go to you for determination some time Monday. Court will now stand in recess until ten o'clock Monday morning.'

Lowell Myers glanced down at the notepads on the table in front of him. He had two days to work on his final argument. It would be a busy—and an immensely important—week-end.

CHAPTER XIII

Monday, 24 January 1972. *The wolf* came howling across Lake Michigan; a bleak, cold wind that rattled the windows of Judge Strayhorn's courtroom. Inside, the jurors filed silently out of the box and moved in single file past a long table that was piled high with the State's evidence. It was all there—the bloody sheets and pillows, the blood-speckled tee-shirt and Donald's trousers with blood on the knees and the tiny, round spot of 'blood-coloured substance' on the seat. Glass vials of blood were on the table and clippings from Earline Brown's fingernails. Glassine envelopes containing bloody strands of hair were there, as well as the victim's sandals with the light brown hair strands embedded in dried blood. The jury members viewed these gruesome exhibits, some with wooden expressions, others with grimaces of distaste, and then they walked slowly back to their seats. When they were all seated, Anthony Corsentino stood up to face them and give the State's closing argument.

'Good morning, ladies and gentlemen. First of all, on behalf of the State of Illinois, we would like to thank you for your attention and your patience. I would also like to thank Mr. Myers at this point ... an extremely courageous and admirable person. He has presented us with an extremely interesting trial. We have seen Mr. Myers, his interpreter, Mrs. Markin, and deaf-mutes courageous enough to come here with interpreters for them ... a case that will go down in what we call jurisprudence history ... no question about it.

'All right. You have heard the evidence. It has come at you fairly fast, and in the last analysis, as in all important things, it seems the little things are the things that count.'

Corsentino detailed the uncontroverted facts—the movement

of Donald Lang on that summer night, from The Bull's Tavern on West Madison Street to the Viceroy Hotel on Warren Boulevard in the company of Earline Brown ...

'It is very important that Earline Brown said to the bartender at Bull's Tavern that she would be right back. This indicates on her part a motive to cheat, like other people have cheated Donald Lang. In other words, take him up to the hotel room, take his money and leave. They go to the hotel ... they go upstairs. Rufus Knight sees them. Rufus Knight has known Donald Lang for thirteen years. There is no question in Donald's mind that somebody has seen him going upstairs. Of course, at this point it is not important. He had no intention of murdering Earline Brown, but it is uncontroverted that he was in that room during the course of the homicide, the murder of Earline Brown. *He was there.*

'First of all, you will be instructed that the State has not proven a motive. We acknowledge this. We have proved no motive. But His Honour will instruct you that we do not have to prove a motive ... only certain requisites ... mental state ... knowledge and intent. The evidence might indicate that Earline Brown wanted to take him for his ten dollars and he got mad, or it might indicate that he wanted to give her only three dollars, and that's where the argument ensued. Donald Lang killed Earline Brown. How? He did it by use of his hands and fists. He also kneed her in the chest and in the neck. More probably he also punched her in the neck and strangled her with his hands; despite the fact that Earline Brown was five-foot ten-inches tall and weighed approximately one hundred and sixty-seven pounds. You have all seen Donald Lang. He is probably no more than five-foot six and one hundred and forty pounds, but Donald Lang has been making his way through the ghetto for the past twenty-five years. Donald Lang has been working at the South Water Market for twelve or thirteen years. Donald Lang does not have an ounce of fat on him. Donald Lang does not like to be cheated. Donald Lang is plenty strong. He can unload a truck, forty thousand pounds of cargo, hundred pound crates in a matter of two to three hours. No question about it, Donald Lang had the capacity and in fact did kill Earline Brown.'

The wind rattled the windows and Anthony Corsentino talked on and on. He talked about the blood on Donald's shirt and pants—not 'flying drops' but smears ... close contact bloodstains—and he talked about the blood on Donald's white socks ...

'The police officers have a conversation and they notice the blood on his socks. Now, Donald Lang we concede cannot hear, but he certainly can sense things. They go outside and what did Donald Lang do? Rolls down the stockings, covering up the blood spots! Evidence that he *knows* he did something wrong and somebody else knows about it!

'Now, what did he do? He draws a picture consisting of stick men. He draws one stick man, indicates that is himself. He draws a stairway, then he draws another stick figure with hair —a woman, Earline Brown. Now, he points to himself and holds up three fingers, then he points to the girl and X's her out. My interpretation is there was a haggle, a disagreement over three dollars as opposed to ten, and he killed her and left.'

Corsentino went over the evidence, piece by piece, analysing the testimony of the various laboratory technicians, placing it all in perspective, making the jury realize how important each and every piece was.

'The technical evidence that was presented was not very interesting ... was not fascinating ... it's cold, scientific evidence that does not lie. But it was very important ... what we call the chain of evidence ... material that was recovered from the scene, from the victim and from the defendant ... a chain of evidence—and that chain has been established. The defendant was arrested because the evidence showed that he clearly did commit the murder of Earline Brown. The day after his arrest, his stepmother, who is apparently concerned with Donald, called the police and turned over to them Donald's tee-shirt. She knows that Donald needs help. And that gets us to the very basis of what is going on here, a jury trial. You are not to be concerned with punishment. We are not seeking the death penalty. We should be hung ourselves if we did in this case because of the defence. But in order for a person in our system to be punished—or to be given treatment, the jury has to turn him over to the Court. This is what we're asking you to do. The disposition, so to speak, of Donald Lang will be left up to the wisdom of His Honour, Judge Strayhorn.'

'Excuse me, Your Honour,' Myers said. 'That is not the purpose of this proceeding. He is not going to be sent to school or anything like that. He is misleading the jury.'

'Objection sustained,' the judge said.

Corsentino continued talking for another forty minutes, and the purpose of his argument was to negate Lowell Myers' interpretation of what had happened in Room 201.

'Let's look at Mr. Myers' opening statement. Earline Brown picks up Donald Lang, that is what Mr. Myers said, and they go to a hotel used by junkies and whores. They had sexual relations. Three men robbed Earline Brown and then murdered her. Blood flying. Earline Brown claws at one of the offenders with her fingernails. Now, evidence has shown that Donald Lang picked up Earline Brown, he was the one looking for prostitutes. They got to a hotel that is in the ghetto, but it really isn't that bad a place. The doors are kept locked after ten at night. There are many permanent residents. It is used by prostitutes, but there is no evidence whatsoever that it is used by drug addicts.

'Now, the contention that Donald Lang had sexual relations with Earline Brown ... the lab reports indicated that she had spermatozoa in the vagina, so I suppose you are to assume that Donald Lang had sexual intercourse with her. Earline Brown was a streetwalker. This was about two o'clock in the morning on a Saturday night. By that time, she had had sexual relations with at least five other people. Secondly, by his own admission, Mr. Myers stated that Donald had his clothes on. How do you have sexual intercourse with your clothes on? Okay, I hate to be offensive, but it is possible, all one has to do is pull his zipper down. Okay ... he had his clothes on. But what about Earline Brown? Did she have sexual intercourse with her hot pants on ... and her girdle on? Her clothes were on her during the course of the assault ... we know that because the clothes were ripped.

'The fingernails of the deceased had blood on them. She was in that closet and her hands were down, and she was bleeding. Of course, there is going to be blood *on top* of her nails. That's how she got the blood on them ... no evidence of any animal or human material underneath those fingernails. That's why Donald Lang did not have any scratches on him!

'We ask you to use your common sense, ladies and gentlemen, in determining the question of reasonable doubt. His Honour has instructed you that the only definition you will get of reasonable doubt is a doubt based on reason. There are no reasonable doubts as to the guilt of the defendant. Mr. Myers said he wanted a fair trial and, of course, a fair verdict.

A fair trial has certainly been accomplished.

'Now, the question of a fair and just verdict. A verdict that is *just* is a verdict of guilty. Thank you.'

Lowell Myers shuffled through his notes. There were many points to cover and not too much time to do it in. An hour ... an hour and a half at the most ... and the future of Donald Lang would be decided, one way or the other.

'You may proceed, Mr. Myers,' Judge Strayhorn said.

Myers put away his notes and walked slowly towards the jury box.

'Ladies and gentlemen of the jury, this has been a long case and a complicated case, but you have all been very patient. This is one of the most unusual cases that was ever heard in a courtroom and if they should ever make a movie out of this case, nobody would believe it. They would think it was fiction that somebody made up. Now, I'm going to speak to you and if anyone cannot hear me, I want them to raise their hand and I will know they are having difficulty.

'Let's talk about Donald. Donald, before he was arrested, was living with his father and his stepmother ... he was working at the South Water Market for Mr. Pullano. Donald had worked at the market for twelve years ... since he was a little boy, and he was a good worker. The prosecutor tried to make it look like Donald is super strong. He can unload a ten thousand pound truck—he's Superman! Go to the A & P ... go to the National or Kroger's, they have ten thousand pound trucks full of groceries that come to the back door and they have high school boys that unload those trucks. It's not that hard ... they use hand trucks ... any high school boy can do it and Donald could do it. Donald is an ordinary working man and he has an ordinary job.

'Now, we have all been together for two weeks and we all know that Donald sometimes has a tough expression on his face. Well, Donald grew up in a neighbourhood that is just boiling with crime. Donald may be strong, but he is small. People are affected by their heights. The little man always feels little. He's a little guy and in his neighbourhood there are men who are much bigger, much stronger. In his neighbourhood there are gangs, and these gangs are very dangerous. Those

176

gangs could grab Donald and take him into an alley, beat him up and take his money ... or his clothes. And if they do that, Donald can't go to a police station. He cannot complain about it. He cannot sign a complaint. He cannot go to court and be a witness. He has no protection. Donald is alone. What can he do? He can act tough, and if he acts tough enough, maybe he will be left alone.

'There was a guard who testified and he said that in the back room Donald is nice. Donald is pleasant. When he's in a place where he does not feel threatened, he's a nice guy. We must understand that Donald feels threatened in this courtroom. This is an unnatural situation for him. Now, actually, if you disregard the expression on his face, Donald has been remarkably patient. He has sat in that chair for two weeks without hearing one word which is the most boring, tedious thing in the world.

'Let's talk about that tavern ... let's talk about that hotel ... a tavern full of prostitutes ... a hotel where prostitutes can rent rooms by the hour. Donald went to that tavern and Earline Brown held up ten fingers ... ten dollars ... and Donald nodded his head up and down and he went with her. The woman took Donald to the Viceroy Hotel and the woman signed the registry card for him because Donald cannot write. Mr. Rufus Knight was in the lobby and he saw that. And then Donald and the woman went up to Room 201. And an hour or so later, Donald comes down. He goes to the telephone and picks it up. He puts the phone down and walks out. He did not report anything to the police. Now, the prosecutor's case is based on three things: Donald was there ... he had blood on him ... and he did not report it to the police. That is the case. There is no evidence that Donald was involved in the fight which took place in that room. So, the question which is presented to you is: Should a man be found guilty of murder if he is in a room where a person is killed and there is blood on him but no particular evidence that he took part in the fight?

'Let's talk about that question. Let's come to grips with it. Suppose you are a man and you are walking down the street with your wife. Some men rush out of an alley and throw you to the ground. They want your wife's wedding ring and they start beating her up and hitting her head on the pavement until they can get the ring off of her finger. They run away and you get up and you pick up your wife and you say "My God!" You run to a tavern and you call the police. Now, should you be arrested for murder? You've got blood on you. You picked up your wife and you've got blood on your stockings. You've got blood on your hands and you wiped some of that blood on your pants. Are the police going to arrest you for murder? Of course not. Why should they arrest you for murder? The blood on you doesn't mean anything. You reported the crime to the police. You have no motive. They're not going to arrest you.

'Let's take another example. Suppose you go to The Bull's Tavern at one o'clock in the morning. You want to get some beer and while you're drinking your beer, this lady comes up to you, Earline Brown. And she says, "For ten dollars, I'll go to a hotel with you." And suppose you say okay ... and you go up to that room at the Viceroy Hotel. After a while, there is a knock on the door. You open the door and some men step into the room. They start talking to Earline. They say, "Earline, where's the stuff?" She says, "Stuff? I gave it to Dolores." And they say, "Dolores said she gave it to you. You've got it and we paid for it. Now, where is it?" There is an argument ... a big fight in that room and you are over by the wall. You don't know what to do. It's a crowded room and you can't get out of it. Now, suppose those men kill the woman. They take her purse and rip it open ... they take her clothes and rip them off. They happen to be looking for something ... for dope, maybe. Finally, they leave. You go down to the lobby and you telephone the police. The police come and you tell them what happened. Would they arrest you for murder? You are there. You've got blood on your stockings. Would they arrest you for murder? No. Why? You reported it. You have no motive. You didn't know the lady. You're a good-working man with a good job. They are not going to arrest you. But, suppose you go down to the lobby and you pick up the telephone and then you think better of it. You don't want to get involved, your wife will kill you. You hang up the telephone and you go home. They pick you up the next day. Are they going to arrest you for murder? Now, it's getting a little bit different. You were there. You've got blood on your socks. You did not report it. Now, it's a borderline case. The police will question you very carefully. If you say I got panicky and ran out, but I didn't do it, I just happened to be in the room when three men killed the lady, the police may believe you. A lot of people get panicky at the scene of a crime. If your background is good, they may let

178

you go. You had no motive. You told the police what happened.

'But now, let's make one more change in the story. Suppose the police pick you up and they say, "Tell us about it." And suppose you do not answer. You say nothing at all. Then, you will be arrested for murder and you will be sitting right there in that chair. They will put you in that chair where Donald is sitting now and prosecute you for murder, not because you had blood on your socks. That's not the real reason. That's not so important. No, the real reason you would be sitting in that chair is because *you would not answer.*

'Now, let's talk about Donald. The police picked him up and they asked him what happened. Donald did not answer. They could tell he was a deaf-mute—or was he? Do you remember Officer Bertucci? He couldn't understand why Donald rolled down his socks. It was his opinion that Donald could hear and speak. They placed him in a line-up and he was identified as being in the hotel the night of the murder. They knew that the blood on him was the woman's blood even though they hadn't tested it yet—but they were pretty sure. They didn't have to release him ... they could have held him until the tests were completed. But no, they let him go ... insufficient evidence, the State's Attorney said ... insufficient evidence. You see, the blood didn't mean anything. It didn't mean that he'd killed the woman. But then they found the registry card. The police asked Mattie Ligon who signed the card. "The man signed it," Mattie Ligon said. "I think the man signed it." And the police took that card and what did they think? If he can read and write, he can communicate. If he can communicate, he was putting on an act yesterday. He's not a deaf-mute. Maybe he can hear, too. He did not have any excuse for not reporting the fight and the killing. That's exactly what happened and Donald was re-arrested and is being prosecuted for murder all because of that card! Now, that is why in this case we have spent half of our time on both sides arguing about whether Donald can communicate because that was the question which brought up the whole case. They thought he was putting on an act and fooling them. And if he did that, then probably he was the murderer. Policemen never like to be fooled. They are human. They resent it. I brought many people into court who testified that Donald cannot hear. He cannot speak ... or read ... or talk ... or communicate in any meaningful way. But the police thought that he could because of that

179

registry card—and some of them still think so.

'Let me explain something. Once a decision is made to prosecute, the case goes forward just like a machine. We have *eight hundred* murder cases a year in Chicago and they handle them just like a factory. Suppose that somewhere along the line a policeman should say ... "I don't see any evidence that he was in a fight. Sure, he was there and he's got a little bit of blood on him, but that doesn't mean anything. Where is the evidence that he killed her?" The other policeman will say, "That's up to the jury. It's not our problem."'

Myers had to pause. It was becoming increasingly difficult for him to speak at great length. His ability to remember how to articulate words was slowly fading. The jury waited patiently for him to resume.

'Now, ladies and gentlemen, we have talked about why this case came up and now we will talk about the case itself. The State is trying to prove that Donald wasn't just a witness, that he was in a fight ... but there is not the slightest proof of that. They have no proof at all and that's quite a problem for them. There is a technique that is called flooding the jury, over-whelming the jury. What you do is, you put a lot of witnesses on the stand and you bring in a lot of evidence ... so much that nobody can keep track of it. If the prosecutor had wanted to, he could have presented his case in three hours. One hour to prove that Donald was there. Simple. We all know that he was there. One hour to prove that her blood was on him. No question about that. One hour to talk about his arrest and to offer proof that he did not report the crime to the police. Three hours. But if the case had been presented to you that way, it would have been a simple case and a simple case would result in a simple answer. So, they flood you with evidence and they flood you with witnesses. What did the crime laboratory men say? I don't think many of you can remember. There was too much there ... too many things. There was blood all over that room and some of that blood fell on some chewing gum wrappers. The prosecution puts them in evidence. What does it mean? Who knows? It means that there was blood thrown around and some of it fell on some garbage. It has no meaning whatever, but it's in evidence. Why? It just makes the case look bigger and more complicated. They found that Donald had some green paint flecks on him and the woman had some green paint flecks on her. So they bring in a scientist to testify about laser beams. It's very impressive, but what does it mean? Donald was with the woman, we all know that. It has no meaning at all, but it adds to the pile. The idea, the technique, is when the pile gets big enough, one juror will say to the other, "Look, is there any evidence he was in a fight?" And the other juror will say, "Look at all that pile of stuff. Maybe there's *something* in there that proves it." You see, you lose track after a while and you tend to assume that because the pile of evidence is so big that there must be something important in there.

'Now, actually, when we go into the evidence carefully, we find that there is a tremendous amount of evidence that proves that Donald was not in any fight—and there *was* a fight. That woman was *beaten* to death. That woman looked like she had gone through fifteen rounds of a prize fight. There was blood all over the place—on the wall, the carpet, the bed. There was a pool of blood in the centre of that bed and it soaked clear through into the box spring. Yes, there was a fight. That woman was big. She was one hundred and sixty pounds ... five feet ten ... and she was a woman who had been in many fights in her life. She knew how to fight. This woman had pointed fingernails and I'm sure she had a reason for having points on them. Women fight with their nails ... they strike for the face ... the eyes. Whoever that woman fought with would have marks on him. There were no marks on Donald Lang. Donald was wearing a thin, white tee-shirt. There were some spots of blood on that shirt, but there is no tear, no rip. If he had been fighting with anyone that person would just naturally grab hold of his tee-shirt at the collar. The collar of a tee-shirt is a nice handle. When a guy is wearing a tee-shirt and gets in a big fight, you invariably find a tear from the collar down. Donald's tee-shirt is not torn in any way, not even a thread is torn. It's in perfect condition.

'Now, ladies and gentlemen, during the years to come, I am sure that all of you are going to think about this case from time to time. You will wonder about it. You will wonder about the strands of hair embedded in the blood on Earline Brown's sandal. Was that hair pulled from someone's head during that woman's last fight? Did the hair fall from her hand on to her shoe? You will wonder about that. I think you will wonder about the drawing. Was Donald trying to explain what took place? Was he trying to express himself? You will wonder.

The police made no attempt to locate or to question the people in the adjoining room ... or the room down the hall. If those people had been brought into court, what would they have said? They might have said plenty. You will wonder about that. You will wonder about the flying drop of blood on the seat of Donald's pants—and it *is* blood even if the drop is too small to test. Maybe it's elephant blood, but my guess is that it's human blood, type "B"—the same as all the other blood. You will wonder about it. You will wonder why Donald picked up that telephone. What did he want to say? There are many different things that you will wonder about.

'The Court will instruct you that if there is a reasonable doubt in your mind about this, you must find Donald Lang not guilty. I cannot tell you what a reasonable doubt is. Every person must decide that for himself. There are two roads you can follow, ladies and gentlemen. One road leads to a guilty verdict ... one road leads to not guilty. I believe that you will follow the road that will lead you to a not guilty verdict. Reasonable doubt ... that rule of law is for the protection of people—and particularly for the protection of handicapped people who may step into a situation which they cannot handle, a situation which is beyond them. And that rule of law is also for the protection of the jury because it protects them against making mistakes.

'My time is almost up. When I am done speaking, the prosecutor will speak to you again and no matter what he might say, I am not allowed to answer. I cannot talk any further. If he says something that I feel is absolutely wrong and I can prove it in black and white, I cannot talk about it. My time is up. Thank you, ladies and gentlemen ... thank you.'

It was Joseph DiNatale's role to play the devil's advocate. That was his job, and thirty-five murder cases a year had honed his courtroom manner to a fine, cutting edge. He looked and acted precisely what he was—a tough State's Attorney. He was also a man with a wife, three kids, and a home in a green and pleasant Chicago suburb. He was a man with a great deal of sympathy and understanding for the frail and the handicapped —one of his children had a serious heart condition—but in the courtroom, he was just a prosecutor pressing for a conviction.

'Ladies and gentlemen,' DiNatale said, 'the hour is late and by now you are tired of hearing speeches. I will try to make mine as brief as possible. I will not indulge in the luxury of

182

thanking you, ladies and gentlemen, because jury duty is not really something you get thanked for. It's kind of like being in the Army. On the day they discharge you no one says thanks. They hand you a piece of paper, and you go on your way. Your thanks, ladies and gentlemen, will be the work that you do in this jury box.

'Now, you have heard from my partner, Mr. Corsentino, and you have heard what I consider to be one of the most brilliant closing arguments I have ever heard in this building from Mr. Myers. It is brilliant in every respect as far as the law, and in his plea for the defendant. It reminds me of when I was a little kid. When I was a kid, we lived in an area which the sociologists today would call a ghetto. When I was a kid, it was called a slum. It was where the Dagos lived, and when I lived in that slum, my grandfather always had a saying. He used to say, "Remember one thing, Joe, we all cry for our own in this world." And that's what Mr. Myers is doing ... he is crying for his own.

'We sympathize and we empathize with him because he has a hearing defect. And that defect puts him and Mr. Lang in a deeper relationship than that of attorney-client. They both suffer the same handicap. They are both members of the same family. And for that reason, they each cry for their own and he has a little greater interest in seeing this man walk out of here than he would if Mr. Lang did not have a handicap. Now, we all cry for our own, and for that reason when the evidence is really not on our side we come armed with the shotgun of imagination. Mr. Myers stands before you and fires volley after volley of shotgun blasts and smoke screens at you. He does this in the hope that one of you will toss aside the evidence and hang your hat on some little thing because, ladies and gentlemen, it is easier to give another human being your sympathy. It is easier to give him a break than it is to do your duty. And Mr. Myers knows that. He is very skilful.

'I don't want to rehash the case with you, I just want to talk about the shotgun blast that was levelled at you. I would like if I may, to clear the smoke out of your eyes. All that you should consider is the evidence that we presented. Mr. Myers presented nothing that would contradict any of the important points of this case. There is not one scintilla of evidence to corroborate the points that he made by his suppositions. We were told how poor Donald lies on the floor on his stomach in the middle of the room while three dastardly, smoke-filled denizens of the deep come from nowhere into this eight-by-ten foot room. We now have five people in that room, and they beat Earline Brown to death—or one of them does while the other two stand idly by doing something or other. Donald lies on his stomach. That's the reason he has blood on the front left knee of his pants and blood on the right knee of his pants and blood on the front of his tee-shirt!

'Now, let's talk about another interesting thing. Counsel went to the scene of the crime. Not on July 26th ... 27th ... or 29th. Not in August ... or September ... or October, but in late November! And in late November, four months after the killing, lo and behold, Counsel sees large spots of blood on what Sarah Williams called just a dirty old carpet. He sees blood on the walls—but the room had been freshly painted. How do you see blood when the walls have been painted? When the carpet has been shampooed? Did he test for blood on the carpet? Did he, in fact, retrieve any swabs so they could be tested by anyone? No. He doesn't know what is on the carpet. It could be ground-in Tootsie Rolls. It could be spilled liquor. It could be some of the dope from the mysterious dope addicts that he sees flying in and out of the Viceroy Hotel. There has been no testimony that the Viceroy Hotel is a habitat of dope addicts. The only testimony we have about dope addicts is unsworn, uncorroborated lawyer talk from a very brilliant and very capable attorney. No question about that, ladies and gentlemen. And I just hope that the common sense we asked you about did not leave you when you heard that very brilliant talk.

'Now, first of all, I don't really pity Donald Lang. I pity his ailment. I pity his impediment, but I don't pity him. He is here before you, ladies and gentlemen, for justice. And it's not only justice for Donald Lang, it's justice for the victim and for society. That is what justice is all about, giving everybody a fair shake. If we let our pity go crazy here and let Donald Lang go loose, that's not really justice. That's pity, and that's pitiable.

'Now, Counsel keeps saying let's be accurate. Well, if we are to be accurate, where, ladies and gentlemen, is the evidence about the three men. Counsel, through his own testimony—and it's not really testimony, because it's not sworn—tells you about three men. There is not any evidence, not one little bit of evidence about three men in this whole case. The only bit

184

of evidence that corroborates anything is the number three. Just the *number* three. That could be three dollars. It could be three acts of intercourse ... it could be three times he strangled and beat her. It could be anything. Counsel, because he cries for his own, chooses to make it *three men*.'

DiNatale stole a quick glance at his wristwatch, a watch that bore the map of Italy engraved on the face. His time for rebuttal was almost up. It was late in the afternoon and the winter night was falling. The wind still rattled the windows and the heat from the radiators was oppressive. The jurors—everyone in the courtroom—showed the strain of a long, hard day.

'Now, how does the blood get on the back of Donald's pants. Okay, he's lying on his stomach. Well, how come the blood is so minute as not to be able to be tested when the blood in *front* is all over. Big spots on the knees ... blood all over the tee-shirt. How does the blood get on them? Does it come up through the carpet by osmosis?

'Now, Donald Lang wasn't rearrested because of the registry card as Counsel would have you believe. He was arrested because the blood on his clothes matched the blood on the victim —type "B". He wasn't picked up the day after the line-up because of the writing on the card. He was picked up three days later because it took a long time to test the victim's blood. It took a long time because she had been thirty-two hours in a closet and they had a hard time at the crime lab getting a positive identification of the blood type.'

'You have five minutes, Mr. DiNatale,' Judge Strayhorn said.

'Thank you, Your Honour. Okay ... it was a Thursday that they matched the blood of the victim to the blood on Donald's clothes, not a Tuesday as Counsel would have you believe. Little things, ladies and gentlemen, they mean a lot.

'Now, why did we put so much stuff in evidence? Because it's the oldest trick in the world. If you don't pull all the evidence in, defence lawyers seize on something and say why didn't they put this in, or that in ... they are hiding something from you. Well, Mr. Corsentino and I are from a different school of prosecutors. We believe in putting it all in and letting it all hang out, as the kids say. Let the jury know everything. Don't hide anything. Be as ethical and as fair as you possibly can. We don't get a bonus if the defendant is found guilty.

'Counsel talked about a big fight in that room. There is not one shred of evidence that there was a fight. Not one. There were no overturned chairs. There was no blood on the walls except one little smear on the wall by the bed. If there was a terrific big fight, where did it happen? In Counsel's mind is where it happened, because that's the only way to walk this defendant out on to the street! Why talk about reasonable inferences when we can make up grandiose fiction. We can use that fiction to talk a guilty man out of the door of this building —but it will not serve the victim ... it will not serve justice. It will serve nothing.

'Mr. Corsentino and I swore a duty to prosecute cases. Counsel has a duty to defend to the best of his ability and to walk his man out of here. You have a duty to hear the evidence. You have a duty to set aside all the arguments, the prejudices, the bias, the sympathy and to come to a decision so that justice is rendered. And you leave the mercy to somebody else. I thank you, ladies and gentlemen, and I feel that if you do your duty, you will have no choice but to return a verdict of guilty. Thank you.'

It was over. There were no more words to be said by the attorneys on either side. It was out of their hands now and in the hands of twelve men and women.

'Members of the jury,' Judge Strayhorn said, 'the evidence and the arguments in the case have been completed and I will now instruct you as to the law ...'

The instructions were lengthy, covering all of Donald's rights as defendant, the basic rules of court procedure and the duty of the jury ...

THE COURT: To sustain the charge of murder, the State must prove the following propositions:

First: That the defendant performed the acts which caused the death of Earline Brown.

Second: That when the defendant did so, he intended to kill or do great bodily harm to Earline Brown.

If you find from your consideration of all the evidence that each of these propositions has been proved beyond a reasonable doubt, then you shall find the defendant guilty ... you should not find the defendant guilty unless the facts and circumstances proved exclude every reasonable theory of innocence.

A recess was then taken and the jury was excused for dinner.

'I think we may have a verdict by seven, seven-thirty,' Judge Strayhorn said. 'If you wish to leave, Mr. Myers ...'

'No,' Myers said. 'I'll stay here.'

The jury deliberated for two hours. Donald Lang was in the lock-up at the rear of the courtroom when the buzzer sounded in the jury room.

'Bring the defendant in,' Judge Strayhorn said.

The court reporter turned to a fresh page and began to write ...

> (Whereupon, the defendant was returned to open court and seated at the counsel table.)

THE COURT: All right. Bring the jury out.

> (Whereupon, the jury was returned to open court and seated in the jury box.)

THE COURT: Be seated, please. Ladies and gentlemen of the jury, have you arrived at a verdict?

JURY FOREMAN: Yes, we have.

THE COURT: Will you pass the verdict to the sheriff. Madam Sheriff, would you pass it to the clerk. Mr. Clerk, would you examine the verdict and find if it's in the proper form.

THE CLERK: I find the verdict in order.

THE COURT: Would you please read the verdict.

THE CLERK: We, the jury, find the defendant, Donald Lang, guilty of murder.

Lowell Myers turned in his chair and looked at Donald. They had been down a long road together and this was where it ended. He frowned and shook his head slowly. Donald stared back at him with an expression of stone.

CHAPTER XIV

Eight hundred murder cases a year. As a judge in the criminal division of the Cook County Circuit Court, the Honourable Earl E. Strayhorn knew how to deal with the guilty. But Donald Lang was outside the realm of his experience. The law itself was cut and dried—any man found guilty of murder in the State of Illinois must serve his term in one of the State's penal institutions. However, it was obvious to Judge Strayhorn that someone like Donald could not be sent to Joliet, Statesville, or any of the other penitentiaries. On 9 February 1972, there was a preliminary hearing in his court to try to determine what institution, if any, was geared to not only confine Lang, but to help him. The hearing was attended by Anthony Corsentino and Lowell Myers.

Myers had decided to withdraw as Donald's attorney. There would be an appeal filed—and a motion for a new trial—but the various appeals and motions would be handled by someone else. After six years, Myers felt that he had done all he could for his client. However, until the new lawyer took over the case, Myers would act on Donald's behalf and serve Judge Strayhorn in an advisory capacity. Both men had the same interest at heart—that Donald Lang be placed in the proper environment. But where would that be?

'Your Honour,' Myers said, 'there is a man here from the Department of Mental Health who is familiar with Donald. He was one of the unit directors at the Dixon School and he will speak to the Court later. He has told me that of all the institutions in the State of Illinois, he feels that *none* of them is suitable. The State Penitentiary is completely unsuitable for somebody with this handicap, and the Dixon State School is no longer suitable. It was at one time, but not any more.

Neither is the Lincoln State School. It is his opinion that the best place for Donald would be the Security Hospital at Chester. Apparently there's been a dramatic change in administration policy there and the Court could order that a special programme be set up for him.'

Merlyn Niedens came forward. He had been the director of Unit V at Dixon for the final two years of Donald Lang's commitment there. He stressed to Judge Strayhorn the special problem they had encountered with Donald ...

'Most of the time, the structure of the unit was basically male and his relationship with the male employees and male residents was quite appropriate ... on most occasions. However, when the programme was changed to a more co-educational set up, we began to have some trouble with Mr. Lang. One of the young ladies in our workshop made a vulgar gesture towards Mr. Lang and he reacted quite violently. Also, during his stay at Dixon, on at least two occasions, young ladies from the security ward came to me and showed me bruises on their bodies which they stated had been afflicted on their persons by Mr. Lang. It was at this time that we changed our opinion. We no longer felt that he could function in a community ... that is to say, in a mixed, co-educational community, that he would need supervision and structure, at least as long as this particular problem persisted. With the type of outbursts that he had, especially towards females, and the open type of situation that we have at Dixon, I don't feel that we have the structure to maintain him there. Frankly, I doubt if there is any institution that has the correct combination of security structure and educational facilities—with the possible exception of the Security Hospital at Chester. The programme there has been revitalized. I have talked to residents who have returned from there and they are most impressed with the new freedoms.'

'Tell me, Mr. Niedens,' Myers said, 'from your experience, would you conclude that Mr. Lang could adjust passively to an all-male atmosphere?'

'Yes. He adjusted well in the cottage, which was all male. Only the workshop was partially made up of females. It was only in the workshop that Mr. Lang had any adjustment problems.'

'So, it is your recommendation that he should be in an all-male environment where he can receive intensive training?'

'Absolutely,' Mr. Niedens said.

'I have just one question,' Corsentino said. 'Are there facilities at this hospital for the teaching and learning of sign language?'

'I couldn't really answer that, because I don't know what the details are of their new programme.'

'Well, I'd take care of that,' Judge Strayhorn said. 'There would have to be established a specialized programme. Before I sentence him, I am going to see that that sort of programme is set forth. To do otherwise, would be to put this man in an atmosphere where he would just vegetate away. I am going to postpone sentencing, and extend the period of time in which post-trial motions can be made. I have had a lengthy conversation with Mr. Myers who is the trial attorney in this matter. It is agreed by Mr. Myers and the Court that this matter is of such a nature in terms of the unique points of law that are involved, that it almost inevitably will end up in the highest Appeal Court in this land.

'Mr. Myers has indicated to me that he does not feel that he should be the proper person to pursue the appellate process and he has, therefore, indicated that he no longer wishes to be considered as the attorny of record. The Court has, of its own motion, decided to appoint Mr. Samuel Adams and Mr. James Montgomery as attorneys in this matter. I will set a hearing date and will direct Mr. Adams and Mr. Montgomery to have present at that hearing officials of the Illinois State penal system. I want these officials to answer questions that I feel I must have answered prior to the imposition of a sentence. Those questions being: What facilities do they have in the entire penal system to take a person with the physical impediment that Mr. Lang has? What means do they have for protecting him in the event that the prison population, or some members of the prison population, did something to him? How would they conduct any necessary hearing in the event a complaint was made by him? How would they be able to understand such a complaint if he made it? All of these things bear on my mind and make me hesitate to sentence Mr. Lang to the general prison system.'

'Your Honour,' Myers said. 'I would like to remain on this case until the time of sentencing.'

'All right.'

'I would also like the Court to hear from a man who used to work with Donald Lang at the Lincoln State School. There are some things that he wants to tell the Court and he came up from Lincoln this morning at his own expense.'

'Fine,' said Judge Strayhorn. 'Swear the witness in, please.'

John Loeffler was not a sociologist, a psychiatrist, a speech therapist nor a lawyer. John Loeffler was simply an elderly man who had worked hard all of his life at physical labour. He had been the maintenance man at the Lincoln State School and Donald Lang had been placed in his care after being transferred from Dixon. John Loeffler's evaluation of Donald Lang as a human being came strictly from the gut—and the heart.

'How long did you work with Donald?' Myers asked.

'About a year.'

'Was he a good worker?'

'He was tops.'

'Was he ever in trouble?'

'Not that I know of.'

'Did he ever give you any problems? Fights ... anything violent?'

'None. We played around ... we kidded ... such like that but nothing serious.'

'Now, Mr. Loeffler, you work at the Lincoln State School and you know Donald. What do you feel that he needs? What do you feel should be done with him?'

'Well ... he should learn more about the sign language. He does seem to know a little but not enough.'

'Do you think that the Lincoln School would be best for him?'

'No. Even if it costs me my job, that place is strictly taboo. It's overcrowded and I don't approve of mixing boys and girls in the same building which is what they are doing. They get together and you've got problems.'

'Just one more question. Where is the best place for Donald to be rehabilitated?'

'Well, I don't know. Maybe some place like Jacksonville where they could teach him something. At Lincoln, they just didn't teach him anything. He was happy there, that I can say. I worked with him and he was happy. A good worker. Couldn't overload him ... the best worker there ever was.'

2 May 1972. The Chicago newspapers were crowded with world-shaking events. The war in Vietnam had become disastrous

for the South Vietnamese. Quang Tri City had fallen and North Vietnamese tanks were racing towards the old Imperial capital of Hue. J. Edgar Hoover died in his sleep that morning, and ninety-one miners died in a silver mine in Kellogg, Idaho. It was on this spring morning that Donald Lang was brought up from the Cook County Jail to Judge Strayhorn's courtroom for sentencing.

Mr. James Slader, a young associate of the law firm of Adams and Montgomery was Donald's attorney. Lowell Myers was in court, as he had promised Judge Strayhorn he would be, and the State's position in the matter would be presented by Assistant State's Attorney James M. Kavanaugh.

'All right,' Judge Strayhorn said when everyone had been assembled. 'This matter has been continued since 24 January when the defendant, Donald Lang, was adjudged guilty of the offence of murder.'

'Your Honour,' James Slader said. 'At this time I would like to call the defendant's trial attorney, Lowell Myers, and ask that he be sworn in and testify on a few matters.'

'You may proceed, Mr. Slader.'

Myers took the witness stand, stated his name and the fact that he had been Donald Lang's attorney on case number 71-2564.

'Mr. Myers,' Slader asked, 'did you attempt, during the course of your representation, to communicate with Mr. Lang?'

'Yes, I did. I tried to communicate with him many times.'

'By what means?'

'In every known way—speaking, writing, drawing pictures, using sign language, pantomime, acting ... everything.'

'Were you at any time able to communicate with him regarding the events that had transpired in the past?'

'No, never. I can communicate about things which are in front of us, about the immediate present, but not about the past.'

'Were you ever able to obtain any explanation of the charges of the indictment of which he has now been convicted?'

'No.'

'Okay, Mr. Myers. Nothing further.'

Slader then faced the Bench. 'Judge, part of our motion for a new trial and motion in arrest of judgment is that the entire structure of the truth-determining process which this court applied, which *all* courts apply, is designed for a person who does not have the handicaps that Donald has. It is the position of the defendant that it is unconstitutional and deprives the defendant of the right to a fair hearing to convict him on the basis of purely circumstantial evidence. The defendant had the benefit of very competent counsel and the benefit of cross-examination, but direct evidence can be either truthful or untruthful, it is either mistaken or accurately recollected. The entire case could have been stipulated to and still there was no defence on the basis of circumstantial evidence, because the one and only way to explain it is for the defendant to get up and say ... yes, those facts are there, but they can also mean something else. What it amounts to, Judge, is that no conviction can constitutionally be based on circumstantial evidence when the defendant is not able to get up and explain that evidence ...

'A number of other issues are raised, Your Honour, but I believe they are adequately covered by our written motion, and I waive any oral argument on them.'

'Mr. State's Attorney?' Judge Strayhorn inquired.

'No comment at this time, Judge.'

'Very well,' Strayhorn said. 'The motion for a new trial will be denied. The motion in arrest of judgment will be denied. We will now proceed to matters in aggravation and mitigation, prior to sentencing.'

State's Attorney Kavanaugh rose and turned to the Bench. 'Your Honour, the defendant, Donald Lang, stands here before this Court, tried by twelve jurors. He has been found guilty of the crime of murder, the most serious crime known to man.

'There has been much comment and conversation in this case concerning Donald Lang's condition, and that Donald Lang is to be looked upon with pity and mercy because of his affliction. Indeed, any rational human being thinks about his affliction with a sense of pity. However, we often neglect to think about the suffering of the victims of crime, in this case, Earline Brown. No comment is usually made about the murdered dead, since they are not around to tell us of the anguish and suffering which occurred to them at the time their life was being taken from them. Earline Brown had a right to live, as much as anybody in this courtroom. And, for that death, which the defendant has been found guilty of beyond a reasonable doubt, the State would recommend to this Court a period of incarceration in the Illinois State Penitentiary for not less than forty nor more than eighty years.'

'Mr. Slader?' the judge said.

'Your Honour,' Slader said. 'We are not asking for pity or mercy from this Court because of Donald's condition. The State attempted to show motive for this alleged murder, that Donald Lang hired the services of a prostitute, that he went to the Viceroy Hotel with her and that she attempted to "rip him off", either to take his money without the service, perhaps to demand more money, or to steal any money that Donald might have had on him. This was the motive the State presented to the jury. Now, they are asking this Court to send him away for forty to eighty years because perhaps he was defending himself.

'Now, here is a man that has been diagnosed all of his life— he has never been really treated, he has just been diagnosed. If he had as much treatment as he had diagnosis, perhaps he wouldn't be here today, perhaps he could have gotten up on the stand and explained what did occur in that room, perhaps it would have amounted to justifiable homicide, or perhaps man-slaughter. We don't know. We are asking the Court to take his inability to defend himself into consideration. Not for mercy, not for pity; he has had too much pity. We are asking the Court to give him the benefit of the doubt ... that he went up there ... that he was about to be ripped off ... that he was defending himself. He could not yell for help. Perhaps it was self-defence and he had to defend himself. He had nowhere to yell to ... no one to yell to ... no way to yell.

'This man may be trainable. We have met in chambers with officials of the Illinois Department of Corrections, and we know that they will set up a programme where Donald may be trained. It may well be that he will never be trained. Everyone who has diagnosed his condition has said that he is untrainable; yet, we know that he can hold a job, we know that this man who is so "untrainable" has learned to live in society, in the ghetto for twenty-five years and hold a job, even though he is totally illiterate. We are dealing with a capable man, we are dealing with a man that needs intensive therapy, but, we are dealing with a man that must return to society before he is an old man. We are dealing with a man that must be given a chance to live and die in society, not in prison. I humbly urge this Court to impose a minimum sentence of fourteen years and a maximum sentence of sixteen years. Thank you.'

'Is there anything else?' Judge Strayhorn asked. 'Does any-one else have anything to say before sentence is imposed?'

'There is a lady,' the clerk said.

The lady was old and black. She stood up in the spectators' seats and, on the Court's direction, walked slowly, hesitantly, to the witness stand.

'Would you state your name, please?'

'My name is Addie May Garson,' the woman said. 'I happen to be Donald's cousin. I think I'm about the oldest one living, you know, since his mother passed, that has known him since he been a little boy. Now, this child was hurt when he was born, he falled out of the baby bed, and he become deaf and dumb. He did go to school for a while, but the teacher said that by him not able to train—which he wasn't potty trained at the time—they couldn't take him in, so they sent him back home. Then, after that, I don't think he had any kind of training or anybody try to teach him to talk, by using the hand signs or the mouth signs, and if he had that kind of training, he would be able to explain exactly what happened in that room. I heard and saw on the TV that he went and drew pictures of different things that went on around here. Well, it looked like maybe someone could interpret those pictures and understand exactly what did take place there. Well, they got money for training young fellows who can't read and who can't talk or help themselves. They is supposed to have some kind of training from somebody. It looks like he could have been put in one of those places where he could have gotten the training so'd he wouldn't be as he is right now. He can't help himself.'

'Thank you, Mrs. Garson,' the judge said. 'Do you have anything else to say?'

'No, sir.'

'Mr. Myers?'

'No, Your Honour. I think all of the points have been covered.'

'Very well. The Court has been in communication with the Department of Corrections. The Court was advised that the penal system in the State of Illinois at this time has no facility where a person of Donald Lang's disability can be placed. The Court concluded that it would be cruel and inhuman punishment to place this defendant in the general prison population. The Court felt that to place him in the general prison population would be placing him as prey to the whims and inhumanity of man to man with no opportunity on his part to communicate anything that happened to him, no ability to complain, no ability to explain anything that had been done to him by others. He would have been nothing more than a cipher who would have been fair game for any cruel prisoner.

'The Court has received communications from many sources, and I am happy at least to feel that as a result of these communications, and the attempts on the part of all persons—Mr. Myers, Mr. Slader, the State's Attorney of Cook County and the Director of Corrections of the State of Illinois—that at least we have a recognition of the fact that this is a special case. There is probably no other case like it in the annals of Anglo-Saxon law. There has certainly never been a case like this ever tried in an American court.

'It is the obligation of the State of Illinois in special problem cases to manufacture and fit a programme to the special needs of problem prisoners. Warden Meeks, of the Joliet Reception and Diagnostic Control Centre, has stated that Donald Lang could be placed in that facility and that a special programme would be designed to teach him to communicate and to prepare him for some form of vocational training, and that every effort would be made to get through that barrier of aphasia which he now suffers. On the representation of Mr. Slader that he has spoken to the officials at North-western University Speech Department and has interested them in attempting to use their expertise in breaking this communication gap, and upon Mr. Meeks' representation that such outside efforts will be acceptable, the Court is going to impose sentence on Donald Lang, even though I am fully aware that what I say he cannot hear, he cannot understand, with the full knowledge that this matter will probably end up before the United States Supreme Court, who will then have the burden of determining whether this is a legally sufficient judgment. It will be the sentence of this court that Donald Lang be taken from the bar of this court and be turned over to the officials of the Department of Correction for eventual incarceration in the Joliet Reception Diagnostic and Special Treatment Centre. I want the record to show that he is not to be removed from that facility without prior approval of this court. I am sentencing him specifically to that facility with the understanding that he is not to be placed in the general prison population as long as he is suffering from his present physical disabilities, for a minimum period of fourteen years and a maximum period not to exceed twenty-five years.'

CHAPTER XV

When the trials were over and Donald's fate was sealed, at least for the foreseeable future, with the turn of the jailer's key, it seemed that the views of him were as disparate as the angles of a shattered prism. There were judges, social workers, relatives, penologists, psychologists, psychiatrists, doctors of medicine, speech therapists and perhaps a dozen others. Each had a special view, a special position.

But who had the total view, the best view? Perhaps the lawyers who both defended and attacked Donald Lang. They certainly had some special insights into his situation. The following are interviews with those lawyers, the prosecutors and the defence. The first was with Joseph Witkowski and Joseph DiNatale, prosecutors for the Ernestine Williams and Earline Brown murder cases. The quotes are verbatim, with the excision of only extraneous material.

DiNatale: A lot of Donald was an act. This is what put me on to it. Corsentino [asst. trial prosecutor] would be making faces at Donald, and Donald would be steaming, making faces back [during preliminary motions, before trial started] and Strayhorn, he's an O.K. judge, but his sense of humour—well, he's a straighty—Donald would go 'Grrrr' and Corsentino would give him the finger, and the judge would say, 'Would you two quit that!' Then Donald would put his hands down at his side. He understood that.

We had a lot of preliminary motions and one day—this one really triggered me—I went up to Donald and told him he was a faker. And he laughed. He started to walk away with the deputy behind him, and Strayhorn—he's a very soft speaker—said, 'Wait a minute. Bring the defendant back.' Donald turned around and came back. And the guard never touched him. Now, either he can read lips, which they claim he can't do, or he heard Strayhorn. And I looked at Myers and Myers looked at me and I started to laugh. And Myers said, 'It's the waves, the sound waves. Sometimes they tingle his ear drums.' I said okay.

But Donald is a sharp kid. I would say he's backward maybe, but street sharp. He compensates. He observes your every move. Donald is so acute, you make the slightest gesture—what do they call it?—body language—you telegraph to him what you're doing.

I have some doubt about the first one—not the second—but the first. But it is Donald's kind of crime. When women are around, he gets hard-ons. You know he's a twenty-five-year-old healthy male, and in tremendous physical condition. He just gets hard-ons. Like I know this guy used to get horny when a pretty girl would walk into the courtroom. I remember one day a black girl with a white outfit, bra-less, came in. Her boy friend was a witness. She was sitting in the front row. He [Donald] never took his eyes off her. He really freaks out when a girl's around. Even some of the bailiffs—even some of the older women. And if a woman's buxom, he goes goofy. Like Shirley [Shirley Thurmond, the prostitute who testified]. He passed her up at the tavern. She was a skinny girl. He didn't like her. Shirley said Donald used to go in the tavern, and he'd go up behind girls and he'd grab their boobs. Behind, as they sat on stools. That's how he'd pick the one he wanted. Shirley was flat, flatter than a board. She was very candid about it. She opened her blouse. 'I don't have anything. That's why he didn't like me.' He was known in the neighbourhood by all the hookers.

This is how they'd settle prices. Donald would go in, feel their boobs. Then he'd bargain [DiNatale illustrates bargaining with his fingers]. I think what really happened—Myers is correct—Earline Brown was going to trick hustle him, because she was a trick hustler. She had a long sheet. She was going to get the ten from Donald, send him into the bathroom and then duck. Because she knew he wouldn't have the courage—or stupidity—to go back to the tavern where her pimp was or he'd maybe get beat up. The first girl (Ernestine Williams) I suspect was probably a streetwalker. She probably did her thing in doorways and alleys. Whereas Earline was strictly a hotel room girl.

Donald I think could just not stand getting stiffed. I went

down to the taverns, and I talked to a few of them. They told me, 'Sure, I've been with the mute ...' with 'Dummy' they called him. 'And he's a real stud. Boy, he comes four, five times without batting an eyelash. And when you tell him, "Hey, one to a trick"—he'd get mad and scream that high-pitched scream, and he'd hit me, so I let him do me four, five times. He's a wild man. Once he gets it up there's no stopping him.' I stopped at the Viceroy Hotel the other day, had coffee with that guy—Rufus Knight. He's sort of a nice old guy. A lonely sort of guy. I don't think he's a doper. He's had a job with Wiebolts (a department store in the Loop) for years and years. If he was pushing dope he wouldn't be living in one room in the Viceroy. He's divorced and goes and sees his family on week-ends. He keeps that Mattie (Ligon, night manager at the Viceroy) company. It's not a bad place, compared to some of the others. It's not what you'd call a ghetto hotel. It's clean, they keep it up, paint the rooms.

That old maid—Sarah, I think (one of the Viceroy Hotel maids, seventy years old). She's a sweetie. The younger one was kind of dumb, but a pretty little girl. When she was on the stand Donald kept licking his lips. She thought he was threatening her, all she could see was his fist. But he was going on like that (gesturing towards his crotch). He was trying to do her. I laughed. I said, 'Anybody got a bag? Donald's really uptight.' I don't mean to be vulgar, but it got to a point during the trial, Donald was really horny because he kept seeing all these women. We had one woman who wasn't too old on the jury, and he'd stare at her when the court was empty.

I sat next to Donald, between him and my partner, because for some reason they couldn't stand each other. My partner he's a physical nut. Another Tarzan. He had to prove himself to everybody.

I'd glance over at Donald and he'd be playing with himself in the courtroom. I mean I really sympathize with him—when it was all over I went to Hanrahan (the State's Attorney) and said, 'I know it's a horrible crime and all, but I can't in all conscience recommend what we call box car figures—a hundred years for this guy. This kid is a sick kid. He probably knows what he did, and what he did was wrong, but he needs to be given a sentence where he can have a hope of getting out and maybe the court can enforce some kind of rehabilitation or school.'

Probably by the time he's forty or maybe thirty-five when he's ready to get out he'll be over this horniness, which is his real bag. I talked with everybody, school, work, he's the hardest worker they ever had. As long as he was in an all-male environment, where everybody carried his own weight, it was O.K. But when he got up into a female society he got really screwed up. And I felt sorry for him. That's why we recommended low, not high. We recommended 30 to 50 and the judge gave him 14 to 25, and we told the judge we wouldn't raise a stink or anything. He'll be out in 11 years 9 months. Could come out in nine.

I had my doubts at first. I'm a little defence-minded. I like to play the devil's advocate. When I went down to the crime lab with Lang, and Myers was there, Myers wanted to see all the exhibits, and being it was Myers, it took six hours. And we had Donald down for handwriting analysis. First Myers tried to get Donald to give one. Then I tried. He just laughed. See, we thought then that he had signed the hotel register, because Mattie Ligon said she thought he had. But later when I talked to Rufus he said no. He was standing where he could see, and Earline signed it. Earline was practically illiterate, that's why the signature looked so goofy. But Donald could mimic some writing. But he couldn't put more than five letters together. Then it would trail off. Because that was as far as they ever got with him in school or at Dixon. I think he could respond with the right therapy. But he'd have to have it forced on him.

WITKOWSKI: One of the psychiatrists I talked to said if they used words like 'money' and things, he understands ...

DINATALE: He even understands Schlitz and all. One day I drew a can with 'Schlitz' and he smiled and raised his hand to his mouth. I think he fakes a little when he gets before the bench because animal instinct makes him know he's in danger. But I don't think he can hear.

WITKOWSKI: It was the most bizarre trial. All these deaf people, translators. The only thing it says about our court system is that we were able to do it, to get through it. At least he had a trial, whatever it was worth.

DINATALE: I tell you the truth. Halfway through the trial I began feeling sorry for Donald. Then towards the end I got unsorry again. I just got the feeling he was faking. You know when his family was there he'd turn around and snicker and make gestures ... like, I'll beat it. He got sort of cocky. He

200

was watching the jury and I think he honestly thought he was a winner. If nothing else, he knows a little about the jury system, he knows what it's about. I think he knew when he was winning. Like the day he refused to come out of the bull pen. I'd see Donald for months getting ready for trial. He'd never squawk, model prisoner. All of a sudden, the day we start selecting the jury, the jury goes to the jury room next to the bull pen and all of a sudden you'd hear the scream and yell. I think he thought if he'd act that way he'd get sympathy. Maybe Myers tipped him off. But the judge tried to keep everybody out of the bull pen. He said he didn't want anybody abusing Donald. You know, in the Cook County Jail they're using Donald as a messenger. He's the best messenger they've ever had. Knows his way around that jail.

I identify with defendants. Maybe I'm different from many of my breed. And I get criticized. But they are the victims of the system. Maybe they don't deserve it—I've had guys who were cold-blooded murderers—I don't think Donald's a cold-blooded murderer, I think he's an impassioned murderer—I mean he's not a *bad* murderer. But the guys who don't have a reason ... I wound up being more sympathetic in the end towards Donald than I was towards Myers. Because Myers, whatever his background is, made it out of his affliction. He didn't have it as bad as Donald Lang and was fortunate enough to live on the North Side and be born white and had people who cared. With Lang they probably just thought he's a dumb kid. I bet every time Donald came home with money his family would route him for half of it. And I'm sure that's one of the reasons that kid is so street smart. He probably had a spot in the neighbourhood where he stashed it. He's just a victim of a system. He's the victim of everybody around him. He doesn't kill men because he respects men and he can deal with them on his own terms. He can't deal with broads. He can't deal with the boobs and the body and the clitoris that controls the male instinct that he can't express. He just can't do it. You gotta feel sorry for a guy like that. Imagine all the men who kill their wives and girl-friends who can speak and are well educated and they still can't deal with problems like that. Imagine this mute whose only women are prostitutes. He just can't adjust to them. I imagine if a woman laughed at Donald Lang he would kill her for laughing at him. Like, a woman can get my goat, not by cursing me or hitting me, by not saying anything and just laughing at me. I get so damn pissed off figuring why she's laughing at me. Donald, he can't express his anger any way but physically.

Where Myers fell down—and I'm a fan of Myers, if I were Lang I would have wanted Myers to represent me—but Myers didn't hammer it home, the silent fury that this kid has to carry around in him that can be triggered. If he had done that I think the jury would have come back with maybe not a not guilty, but with a reduced charge. That plus the fact that we had a weak case, a circumstantial case, might have gotten him a not guilty or a lesser verdict. This was pure circumstance ... And of course we introduced subtly the fact that he couldn't be let out on the streets again. He had to be controlled.

One of the things that turned the tide for us, we argued to the jury, 'You have nothing to do with the sentence. Just say guilty or not guilty.' If that had been a typical black on black case, if Donald could speak, he would have taken the stand and said, 'She trick hustled me, she got me mad, she was just as big as me, she pushed me, I got pissed and I choked her. I'm sorry I did it.' A typical jury would have found him guilty of manslaughter or would have walked him out.

I don't think that jury cast any kind of stones at him because of the whores. I think they understood this was the only kind of woman he could make it with. If he could have told his story, we couldn't have rebutted that.

There were only two people in that hotel room. Or he might have said, 'Look, I was there, I had intercourse with her and I left. And maybe three other guys came in and did her in.' And the most he'd get is manslaughter.

We got a lucky break because many of Myers' expert witnesses lied on the stand. I think they tried to do what so many state witnesses do—they colour the truth. And that reflected on Myers. They try too much to help, and then they don't admit when they're wrong. Like that one, the deaf expert. I thought I'd throw a shot at him—could Donald have drawn a picture of a camper? He said definitely not—and we'd just heard from Donald's employer that that's how he described the camper. It destroyed credibility.

I don't think anybody could have done a better job than Myers. He was on good ground. I think one of the things that tripped him up was that the jury observed Donald, and they just couldn't believe Donald was that handicapped.

I think it was a mistake bringing in whether Donald could understand. But I don't think any other attorney could have come as close to pulling it off as Myers did. I admired the way he put that case together. He is a good poker player. He said let them get all that evidence in, because it doesn't prove anything. And I think from his theory he was right. The legal part was right. The jury just didn't believe it about Donald.

A few times, Myers appealed to the jury's white dislike for black people. Like he tried to dirty up Earline—which I think was a mistake. She was a prostitute but she's dead. You know, juries don't like you to dirty up a dead person—even if she's a tramp. I don't blame him really, because that was an element of his case that she was up there to trick Donald. I really don't think it was anything Myers did. Mattie Ligon and Rufus Knight—he's a short, round guy, looks kind of like a porter on a train—kind of a guy white people instinctively like—he came across too good. Whether he's dirty or not, if you can't prove it, you better lay off. Myers brought all his records in, and he was clean. Had held that department store job 15 years.

The Illinois Supreme Court created this monster because they didn't have the guts in 1965 to do something about it. If they had, Donald Lang would never have killed this girl. Should have made a recommendation to the legislature to get the ball rolling. They knew then the issue was physical rather than mental incompetence. They hinted at it in their opinion. We can't rule on the question now, is what they said. Wait until he's tried and convicted. In other words, what they're really saying is wait until he kills somebody else and is tried again, and then you bring it back for us and then we'll rule on it. That's what Strayhorn said. 'They tied my hands.' It really bothered him. You have no idea of the work he personally put in with us, after the case was over, trying to figure out what we could do about it.

WITKOWSKI: If anybody's looking for someone to blame on this, it has to be the Department of Mental Health. He could have responded to treatment, if they'd put in the time. Maybe they don't have the money, but ... and now they're going to do it—try to train this guy.

DiNATALE: I think on the first case what may have happened, Donald ran afoul of her pimp and he was the one who did her in. Because Donald Lang was the kind of guy pimps liked to abuse. They'd say, 'Gimme the money' and run off, and not even give him the dignity of a trick hustle.

Strayhorn was really surprised when we pulled off a conviction in this second case. When you get the case down to its essentials, we really had nothing. They better do a damn good job with Donald, because he's coming out in a few years.

You know, I laughed when I heard about the case, what we'd have to go through with it. Sure enough, I was in another courtroom and I got transferred and the case was there, waiting for me like a bad dream.

One other thing, Myers may have overplayed his routine. He would have done better if he'd struggled a little bit, to make it look as if he was trying to be in their world, rather than making them come into his. As I sat there I said to myself, 'Be detached. Try to think what the jurors think.' And the first thing that came to me is Myers is too busy being deaf, making the jury do everything his way. It was a hard trial. There were parts where there was me asking questions of a witness, a deaf-mute, and a translator translating what the answer was from the deaf-mute to me, and Myers had his own translator—it began after a while to wear on the jury that they had to go so much into his world. Maybe if he hadn't been so efficient—if he'd struggled a little more. Because everything he did was efficient, but efficient in his world. Know what I mean? He would have had more effect if he'd been inefficient, but in our world. That would have made the difference, and gotten the sympathy.

After two weeks of watching this guy operate like a machine, at the summary all of a sudden he was more—sympathetic, all alone. What if he'd said during the trial—'Judge, may we have a sidebar? I didn't get all that. I couldn't make all of that out?' Keep it in front of that jury, with lots of women. Maybe—well, maybe if he'd played on his disability more. A lot of lawyers win their cases that way—by being dramatic. By being a show-man rather than a lawyer. Of course, he might have had to compromise himself to do that.

Losers are less expansive than winners. Lowell Myers said:

'If Donald had been given a little education *at the proper time* it would have made all the difference in the world.

'He was given no help at all—and was left to wander around

in the black ghetto of Chicago. I think everyone will agree it's a pity and a shame.'

Donald Lang is in the Cook County Jail, Chicago, Illinois. Judge Strayhorn and the prison superintendent felt that he would be better off there than at Joliet, mainly because of the proximity to the North-western University Speech and Hearing Clinic. Dr. Helmer Myklebust is no longer associated with the university, so there is no one at North-western who has any prior experience in testing, or treating, Donald. He goes to school in the morning and works during the afternoon. 'School' consists of the efforts of a good-hearted social worker to teach him sign language. It hardly qualifies as the 'special programme ... designed to teach him to communicate ...' designated by Judge Strayhorn.

Nevertheless, Donald has an active life at the jail, where the other inmates seem to accept and like him, and the prison officials show concern about what happens to him. The guards have chipped in to give him spending money for cigarettes, etc.

Donald has his own cell and almost the complete run of the prison. Warden Nathaniel Brown, a former teacher of handicapped children and a YMCA street worker, has taken Donald under his wing.

'He's the hardest worker in the place,' Brown says. 'You can get him to do anything, from mowing the lawn to running errands.' Warden Brown believes that one of the reasons Donald rejected earlier efforts to teach him was that he didn't respect the teachers.

Donald can recognize numbers easily now. If Warden Brown wishes to send a message to any part of the prison, he writes a number on a piece of paper, hands Donald the message, and Donald runs it to the proper cell tier or office. He never makes a mistake.

Donald selects certain people—always men—to respect. A guard at Cook County Jail is one. Warden Brown is another. 'He watches how other men treat each other,' says Brown. 'He doesn't miss anything—his eyes are very sharp.'

Lowell Myers? Warden Brown remembers that early in the trial Donald would indicate when he wanted to 'talk' with Lowell by making rings around his eyes with his fingers, simulating the hornrimmed glasses Lowell wore. Donald also wants a 'hearing' aid. Lowell wears one.

It may well be that the case of Donald Lang will one day be heard before the United States Supreme Court. It may well be that the charges against him will be dismissed. Donald Lang knows nothing about such matters. He runs his errands and drives his lawn mower. He is a working man, a functioning man. One day, perhaps—if it is not too late—a way may be found to release him from the prison, the solitary confinement, in which he has been forced to spend his whole life.

AUTHOR'S NOTE

There has been some protest to me about my choice of title for this book. Some of it from groups who work for the deaf and the mute. I have responded that the choice was deliberate —the cruellest, most shocking and seemingly irresponsible labelling of Donald Lang. This is how he and his handicaps were labelled and ignored—cruelly, shockingly, irresponsibly—from his childhood.

If in the shock there comes some awareness of the real cruelty and social irresponsibility, we might see the day when the label is expunged and its victims somehow helped to escape it.